TIANANMEN 1989
OUR SHATTERED HOPES

WRITTEN BY **LUN ZHANG**
AND **ADRIEN GOMBEAUD**
ART BY **AMEZIANE**

Dramatis Personæ
The Primary Players in the Spring of 1989 in Beijing

In addition to the real-life figures listed below, the creators have added fictional characters (students, restaurateurs, journalists, etc.) as needed for the purposes of this story.

THE STUDENT MOVEMENT

Chai Ling

Born in 1966. Once a model member of the Communist Youth League of China. In 1989, she was a student at Beijing Normal University. After the spring of 1989, she fled to the U.S. A graduate of Princeton and Harvard, she founded Jenzabar Inc., a company providing education software and services to universities. Having converted to Christianity, she runs All Girls Allowed, an organization dedicated to ending China's one-child policy and its resulting abortions.

Liu Gang

Born in 1961. In 1989, this former physics student at Peking University became a pro-democracy activist with no official job. Arrested on June 15, 1989, he was sentenced to six years in prison. Freed in 1996, he moved to the U.S., where he pursued studies at Columbia University in New York. Though he continued to be involved in the struggle for democracy in China, he focused his research on computer science, later becoming a Wall Street analyst for the Morgan Stanley investment bank.

Wang Chaohua

Born in 1952. In 1989, she finished her third year at the Chinese Academy of Social Sciences. She managed to flee eight months after the events in Beijing, and reached the U.S., where she finished a dissertation on Chinese literature at the University of California, Los Angeles. She is now an independent writer and researcher. Her subjects include intellectual life in China.

Wang Dan

Born in 1969. In 1989, he was a student in the Department of History at Peking University. On July 2, he was arrested and sentenced to four years in prison. Freed in 1993, he was arrested again in 1995 and sentenced to 11 years in prison the following year. He was released in 1998 for medical reasons, and exiled to the U.S., where he obtained a Ph.D. in East Asian History from Harvard. After teaching in Taiwan for eight years, he now lives in the U.S. once more.

Wu'er Kaixi

Born in 1968. In 1989, he was a student at Beijing Normal University. Following Tiananmen, he fled to France, and then the U.S., where he began studies at Harvard, leaving after one year. He then moved to Taiwan, where he became a journalist and entrepreneur.

THE INTELLECTUALS

Chen Ziming

Born in 1952. A chemist by training, he and Wang Juntao helped found the Beijing Social and Economic Sciences Research Institute. He also published an influential periodical, *Economics Weekly*. Imprisoned once in 1975, he was arrested again in 1989 and sentenced to 13 years in prison. Released in 1994, he was arrested once more in 1995, then allowed to finish his sentence under house arrest in 1996. He continued to be active throughout his life, publishing articles online under various pen names. He died of cancer in Beijing in 2014.

Liu Xiaobo

Born in 1955. Literature professor at Beijing Normal University. In 1989, Columbia University invited him to New York. He returned to Beijing during the Tiananmen protests. On June 6, he was arrested and imprisoned for a year and a half. Sentenced to a labor camp in 1996 following his activities supporting democracy in China, he was released in 1999. In 2008, he participated in writing the Charter 08, a manifesto signed by over 300 intellectuals calling for the establishment of democracy in China. In 2009, he was sentenced to 11 years in prison. The following year, he received the Nobel Peace Prize, which he dedicated from his prison cell to "the Tiananmen martyrs." Diagnosed with cancer, he was granted medical parole on June 26, 2017. He died on July 13 at a hospital in Shenyang. Several of his books have been translated in English, including *June Fourth Elegies: Poems* translated from the Chinese by Jeffrey Yang (Graywolf Press, 2012).

Wang Juntao

Born in 1958. Former activist at the Democracy Wall, he edited several political publications, and with Chen Ziming, helped found the Beijing Social and Economic Sciences Research Institute. After four months on the run, he was arrested in the city of Changsha. Sentenced to 13 years in prison, he was freed in 1994 at the request of international human rights organizations and President Clinton. After graduating from Harvard, he went on to write a dissertation in political science at Columbia in 2006. He now lives in New Jersey, where he keeps up the fight for democracy in China as president of the Democracy in China party.

THE BUSINESSMAN

Wan Runnan

Born in 1946. An engineer by training and a graduate of Tsinghua University, he founded the Stone Corporation, China's first software company, in 1984. In the wake of reform policies, the company expanded, opening offices in several countries. In 1989, Wan Runnan was also General Secretary of the National Association of Private Entrepreneurs. The Stone Corporation became the student movement's most significant economic supporter. After the repression, he was exiled to France, where he invested in a restaurant in the Halles district of Paris for a while. With other exiled intellectuals and activists, he founded the Federation for a Democratic China.

THE SINGER

Cui Jian

Born in 1961. The son of musicians, he started China's first rock group in 1984. In 1989, his second Rock' n' Roll album about the Long March was a huge hit. His 1989 song "Nothing to My Name," written five years earlier, became one of the anthems of Tiananmen, and he appeared with the students. After a career of more than 30 years, the father of Chinese rock is now an icon and the voice of a generation.

THE CHINESE COMMUNIST PARTY

Deng Xiaoping

Born in 1904. A famous member of the Communist Party, he took part in the Long March, and held various important offices during the 1950s. Purged during the Cultural Revolution, he was rehabilitated after Mao Zedong's death, and instituted economic reforms in the 1980s. In 1989, he was officially only in charge of the Central Military Commission, but in reality, the "Little Helmsman" retained a firm hold on power. After the repression, he relaunched his reform policies in 1992, laying the foundation for modern China's economic development. He died in 1997.

Li Peng

Born in 1928. The adopted son of Zhou Enlai, he was trained as an engineer and became a career Party member. This ultraconservative became Prime Minister in 1987, just as reformer Zhao Ziyang was named the Party's Secretary-General. He both supported and participated in the 1989 repression and remained Prime Minister until 1998.

Yang Shangkun

Born in 1907. A veteran of the Long March, he was imprisoned during the Cultural Revolution. After Mao's death, he rose to power on Deng Xiaoping's coattails. In 1988, he became President of the People's Republic of China. His influence with the armed forces increased so greatly after the repression that Deng Xiaoping forced him to step down in 1993. He handed over his position to Jiang Zemin and died in 1998.

Zhao Ziyang

Born in 1919. Party member since 1938, veteran of the People's Liberation Army, and victim of the Red Guard during the Cultural Revolution. Rehabilitated in 1971, he became Prime Minister in 1980, and made market-oriented economic reforms. In 1987, he succeeded Hu Yaobang at the head of the Communist Party. In the spring of 1989, he advocated dialogue with the students. He was ousted and placed under house arrest until his death in 2004. His memoirs, *Prisoner of the State*, were published in English in 2009.

Hu Yaobang

Born in 1915. A veteran of the Long March, he held various positions at local and national levels in the 1950s, before being ousted from power during the Cultural Revolution. Once back on the scene in the 1970s, he rehabilitated the intellectuals who were victims of the 1960s purges. He became General Secretary of the Party in 1980, where he implemented a reform policy. Deemed responsible for the pro-democratic demonstrations in 1986, he was forced to resign. His death on April 15, 1989 would be one of the inciting incidents for the Tiananmen movement.

Yan Mingfu

Born in 1931. As Mao Zedong's personal Russian interpreter, he held various high positions during the 1950s before being accused of espionage and imprisoned during the Cultural Revolution. He returned to the spotlight in 1985 by taking charge of the United Front Work Department of the Communist Party's Central Secretariat. During the events of 1989, he and Zhao Ziyang attempted to foster dialogue between the Party and the demonstrators. Removed from power after the massacre, he returned briefly to politics in 1991 as the vice minister of Civil Affairs, coordinating philanthropic activities in China. His daughter Yan Lan has written a history of their family, *The House of Yan* forthcoming in English (Harper, 2020).

The pages that follow are not an autobiography, exactly, but rather the story of a man who had a life very much like mine. This fictional twin lived through the same events, in a dramatized and thus necessarily condensed fashion. Told in such a way, this story is not only my own, but that of millions of Chinese people who experienced these events, both in Beijing and throughout the world.

I was but a humble participant, witness to a vast collective movement. The true heroes of Tiananmen will forever remain the student hunger strikers as well as all the nameless people of Beijing whose stood up to the rifles and the tanks, to protect the students and defend a great cause. As the story of one who survived, this book is first and foremost a tribute to those who did not.

I hereby dedicate it to my three children, who grew up in France. Thirty years after Tiananmen, I am sharing my story with them, so that they will understand the journey I have made. I am sharing it with readers young and old, who wish to learn more about these events that upended the fate of a great people, with whom they will be sharing their future.

Lun Zhang, Paris, Fall 2018

I LEFT CHINA THIRTY YEARS AGO.

AND YET, NOT A DAY GOES BY THAT I DON'T GO BACK TO TIANANMEN SQUARE.

YOU MIGHT NOT HAVE HEARD OF THE PLACE I'M TALKING ABOUT.

I MEAN TIANANMEN AS IT WAS IN THE '80S. A VAST, SERENE STRETCH OF GRANITE THE SIZE OF AN AIRPORT, BENEATH A SKY DOTTED WITH PIGEONS AND KITES.

5

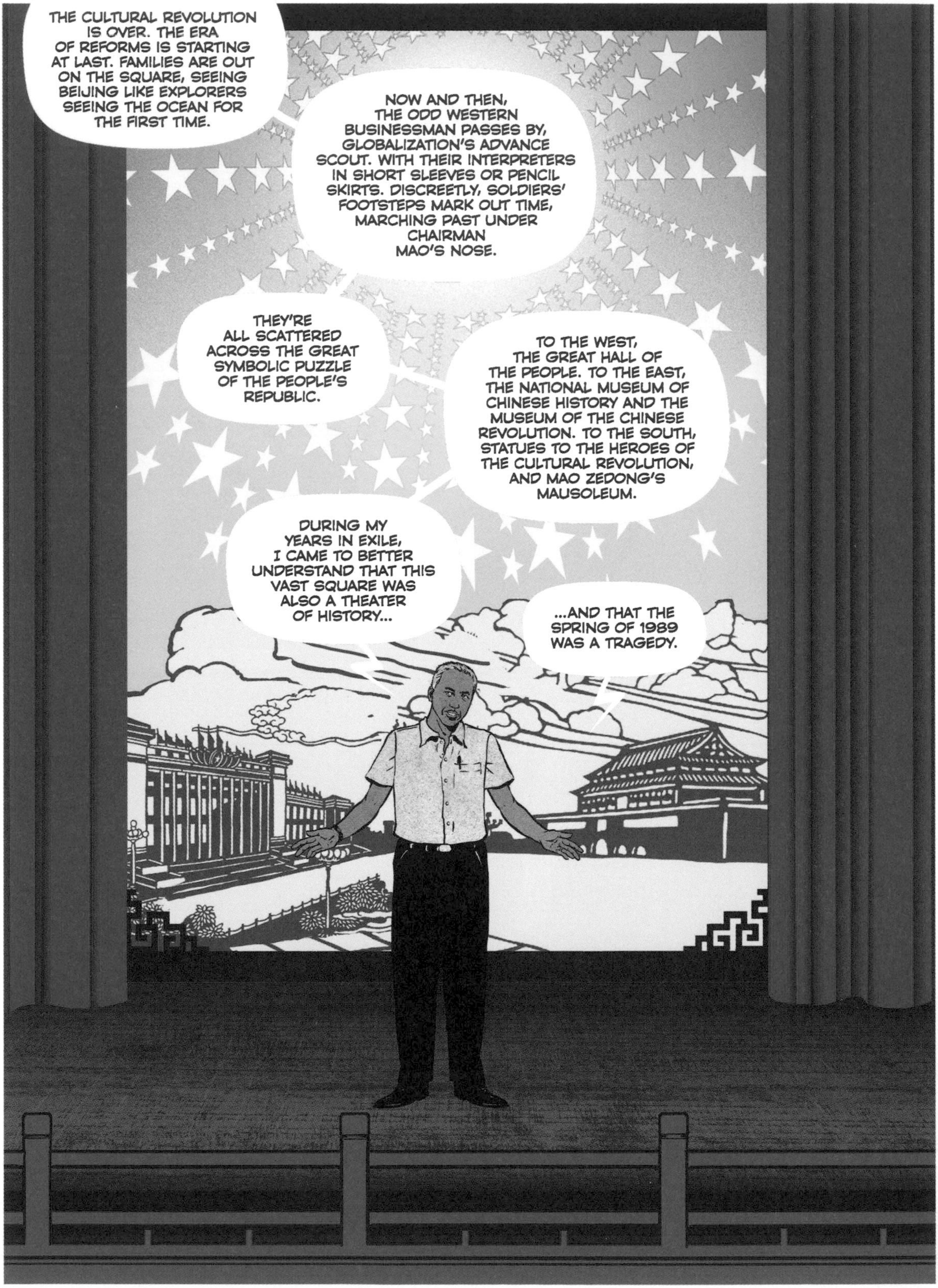
THE CULTURAL REVOLUTION IS OVER. THE ERA OF REFORMS IS STARTING AT LAST. FAMILIES ARE OUT ON THE SQUARE, SEEING BEIJING LIKE EXPLORERS SEEING THE OCEAN FOR THE FIRST TIME.
NOW AND THEN, THE ODD WESTERN BUSINESSMAN PASSES BY, GLOBALIZATION'S ADVANCE SCOUT. WITH THEIR INTERPRETERS IN SHORT SLEEVES OR PENCIL SKIRTS. DISCREETLY, SOLDIERS' FOOTSTEPS MARK OUT TIME, MARCHING PAST UNDER CHAIRMAN MAO'S NOSE.
THEY'RE ALL SCATTERED ACROSS THE GREAT SYMBOLIC PUZZLE OF THE PEOPLE'S REPUBLIC.
TO THE WEST, THE GREAT HALL OF THE PEOPLE. TO THE EAST, THE NATIONAL MUSEUM OF CHINESE HISTORY AND THE MUSEUM OF THE CHINESE REVOLUTION. TO THE SOUTH, STATUES TO THE HEROES OF THE CULTURAL REVOLUTION, AND MAO ZEDONG'S MAUSOLEUM.
DURING MY YEARS IN EXILE, I CAME TO BETTER UNDERSTAND THAT THIS VAST SQUARE WAS ALSO A THEATER OF HISTORY...
...AND THAT THE SPRING OF 1989 WAS A TRAGEDY.

ACT I
-THE YEARS OF OPENING-

I WAS BORN IN SHENYANG, IN NORTHERN CHINA. IN THE LATE 1950S, THE "GREAT LEAP FORWARD" HAD LAID WASTE TO THE ECONOMY AND CAUSED A MASSIVE FAMINE ACROSS THE LAND. TO GET THE UPPER HAND OVER HIS DETRACTORS, MAO LAUNCHED THE CULTURAL REVOLUTION IN 1966, A NEW AND BLOODY UTOPIA MEANT TO EFFACE ALL THE "OLDS" OF THE FORMER WORLD WITH STAGGERING VIOLENCE.

MY PARENTS, "INTELLECTUAL CADRE," WERE AMONG THIS MOVEMENT'S TARGETS AND HAD TO BE "REEDUCATED" BY THE PEASANTRY. SO I HAVE A VERY VIVID MEMORY OF OUR FORCED DEPARTURE FOR THE COUNTRYSIDE ONE WINTER MORNING IN 1969.

THE FAMILIES WERE HERDED INTO BUSES, OUR PERSONAL EFFECTS JOSTLING ALONG BEHIND US IN A CONVOY OF TRUCKS. LATE THAT NIGHT, WE ARRIVED SOMEWHERE NEAR PANJIN. THIS WAS WHERE I WOULD NOW GROW UP, AMIDST THE FIELDS.

I WAS EIGHT.

MAO WAS OUR GUIDE AND THE VILLAGE STABLE OUR CLASSROOM. WHEN I WASN'T STUDYING, I PLANTED RICE.

IN 1971, A PLANE CRASHED IN THE MONGOLIAN STEPPES. THERE WERE NO SURVIVORS. ON BOARD WERE GENERAL LIN BIAO, MAO'S RIGHT ARM, HEADING FOR THE USSR. NO DOUBT HE WAS FLEEING YET ANOTHER PURGE HIS MASTER HAD ORCHESTRATED... NEVERTHELESS, AFTER HIS DEATH, THE CULTURAL REVOLUTION REACHED A TURNING POINT, AND A FEW EXILED FAMILIES WERE ABLE TO RETURN HOME.

* STUDY DILIGENTLY AND MAKE PROGRESS DAILY.

AFTER THE FIELDS, WE WENT BACK TO SHENYANG.

THEN CAME SEPTEMBER 9, 1976.

WE LEARNED OF OUR ALMIGHTY CHAIRMAN'S DEATH. HE HAD STEERED CHINA FOR OVER 25 YEARS. DESPITE THE POVERTY, THE PAIN, THE TEARS, AND THE PRIVATION, THAT DAY ALL CHINA WAS AT A LOSS.

IN THE STREETS AND THE AVENUES, THE FACTORIES AND THE FIELDS, EVERYONE WEPT OVER THE PASSING OF THE GREAT HELMSMAN.

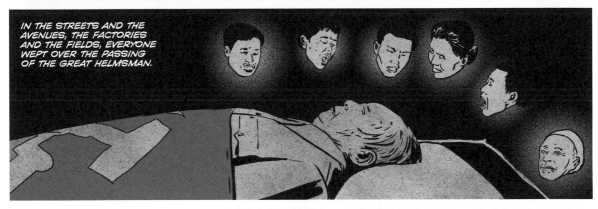

ON OCTOBER 6, HIS WIFE JIANG QING AND HER "GANG OF FOUR" WERE ARRESTED. NO ONE CRIED ABOUT THAT.

坚决打倒王张江姚反党集团!

LATER, THEY WOULD BE TRIED AND SEVERELY PUNISHED FOR THEIR CRIMES.

MEANWHILE, THE CULTURAL REVOLUTION HAD TAKEN ITS TOLL. JUST HOW MANY LIVES WERE LOST, WE MAY NEVER KNOW, BUT IT IS ESTIMATED TO BE IN THE MILLIONS.

IN A FEW YEARS,
THE FACE OF CHINA
CHANGED.

IN THE STREETS,
CLOTHES TOOK ON COLOR.
I WAS ASTONISHED TO SEE
IMPROMPTU DANCES BEING
HELD IN THE PARKS. THE
DARKNESS OF THE 1970S
SOON FADED INTO THE
DISTANCE.

IN SCHOOLS AND COLLEGES
ONCE AGAIN, CHINA'S YOUTH
COULD RESUME THEIR STUDIES.

IN 1984, I WATCHED ON TV AS A CROWD OF STUDENTS GATHERED ON CHANG'AN AVENUE AND TIANANMEN
SQUARE IN BEIJING.

IN THE VERY SPOT WHERE CROWDS HAD ONCE MOURNED MAO'S DEATH, ANOTHER HAD SPONTANEOUSLY
FORMED TO HAIL THE RETURN OF ITS NEW LEADER. "HELLO, XIAOPING!" PROCLAIMED THEIR SIGNS.

AN HISTORIC LEADER LONG KEPT FROM POWER AND EXILED TO DISTANT
PROVINCES, DENG XIAOPING WAS NOW TAKING THE COUNTRY'S REINS
AND LAUNCHING A NEW, UNPRECEDENTED REFORM POLICY.

A NEW DAY WAS DAWNING FOR CHINA. AND FOR MYSELF, AS WELL.
ONE YEAR LATER, I GOT ON A PACKED TRAIN HEADED FOR THE CAPITAL.

OUT THE WINDOW, I GLIMPSED FIELDS BEING PLOWED, THE CHIMNEYS OF
BUSTLING FACTORIES... LANDSCAPES OF AN ECONOMY ON THE UPSWING.

AFTER AN ECONOMICS
DEGREE, I BRIEFLY
WORKED FOR A
CHEMICAL CONCERN.

IN BEIJING, I INTENDED TO
SWITCH TRACKS: PICK UP MY
SOCIOLOGY STUDIES AGAIN TO
BECOME A PROFESSOR AND, AS
AN INTELLECTUAL, TAKE PART IN
THE REFORMS CONTRIBUTING
TO MY COUNTRY'S PROGRESS.

THERE'S ME, IN THE SECOND HALF OF THE '80S: A YOUNG UNIVERSITY PROFESSOR.

I LOVED THE CAREFEE BEIJING SUMMERS, NOW LONG SINCE VANISHED. WITH THE OPENING OF THE ECONOMY, A THOUSAND LITTLE TRADES HAD BLOSSOMED ON THE SIDEWALKS. DENG XIAOPING ENCOURAGED THE CHINESE TO "BREAK THEIR IRON RICE BOWLS", THE MAOIST TERM FOR OCCUPATIONS WITH GUARANTEED JOB SECURITY, STEADY INCOME, AND BENEFITS. THE CITY BECAME A GREAT WORKSHOP AND IMPROVISED MARKETPLACE.

李记饺子

* LI'S DUMPLINGS

THESE REFORMS ARE GOOD.

OPENING OUR OWN SHOPS, DIVING INTO THE SEA OF BUSINESS...

BUT IF THE PRICE OF FLOUR KEEPS GOING UP...

DUMPLINGS WILL BECOME A RICH MAN'S FOOD!

AND AT THIS PACE, WE'LL STILL BE WATCHING COLOR TV THROUGH THE NEIGHBOR'S WINDOW!

1986

THE PARTY URGED THE PEOPLE TO START THEIR OWN BUSINESSES. BUT THE RISING PRICES SEEMED BEYOND CONTROL...

STILL, SOME MADE OUT BETTER THAN OTHERS UNDER THE REFORMS.

IT WAS BLINDINGLY OBVIOUS, AND FILLED US WITH RAGE. CORRUPTION RULED THE ERA. FACED WITH SUCH INJUSTICE, OUR FURY GREW.

AND SO, ALMOST EVERY YEAR, WE GATHERED IN TIANANMEN SQUARE.

MORE OR LESS CONSCIOUSLY, WE WERE CONTINUING A VAST MOVEMENT THAT HAD TAKEN ROOT A GOOD DOZEN YEARS EARLIER, WEST OF TIANANMEN, IN XIDAN STREET.

IN NOVEMBER 1978, THE NEW REFORMISTS IN POWER ENCOURAGED CRITIQUE OF THE CULTURAL REVOLUTION.

SPONTANEOUSLY, BEIJING PEOPLE BEGAN TO POST THEIR GRIEVANCES AND COMPLAINTS ON AN OLD BRICK WALL.

THE STREET SOON BECAME A FORUM, AND "DEMOCRACY WALL" WAS COVERED WITH BIG-CHARACTER POSTERS: THE DAZIBAOS, CRITICIZING MAO'S DICTATORSHIP, CALLING FOR GREATER FREEDOM, AND EVEN PROPOSING A "DECLARATION OF HUMAN RIGHTS IN CHINA."

AT THE TIME, DENG XIAOPING HAD JUST DECLARED THE ADVENT OF THE "FOUR MODERNIZATIONS":

AGRICULTURE   INDUSTRY   NATIONAL DEFENSE   SCIENCE AND TECHNOLOGY

WEI JINGSHENG WAS 28, THE SON OF AN EDUCATED FAMILY CLOSE TO PARTY LEADERS. HE HIMSELF HAD BEEN IN THE RED GUARD. ON DECEMBER 5, 1979, HE HAD DARED TO PROPOSE A FIFTH MODERNIZATION.

THE FIFTH MODERNIZATION MUST BE: DEMOCRACY!

THE EVENTS OF 1989 WOULD REACH HIM ONLY AS A WHISPER, DEEP IN HIS CELL. FREED IN 1993 WEI JINGSHENG WOULD BE ARRESTED AGAIN ONE YEAR LATER, THEN DEPORTED TO THE U.S. IN 1997.

IN EARLY 1987, A FEW THOUSAND OF US DEMONSTRATED IN THE SNOW AND THE PIERCING SIBERIAN WIND. THAT NIGHT, MORE THAN EIGHTY PEOPLE WERE ARRESTED.

OUR BANNERS PROCLAIMED THE SAME SLOGANS, OVER AND OVER: "DOWN WITH CORRUPTION!" "DEMOCRACY!"

FOR MONTHS NOW, PROTESTS AND MARCHES HAD MULTIPLIED. I FELT THE STREETS PLAYING A SYMPHONY SOON TO REACH CRESCENDO.

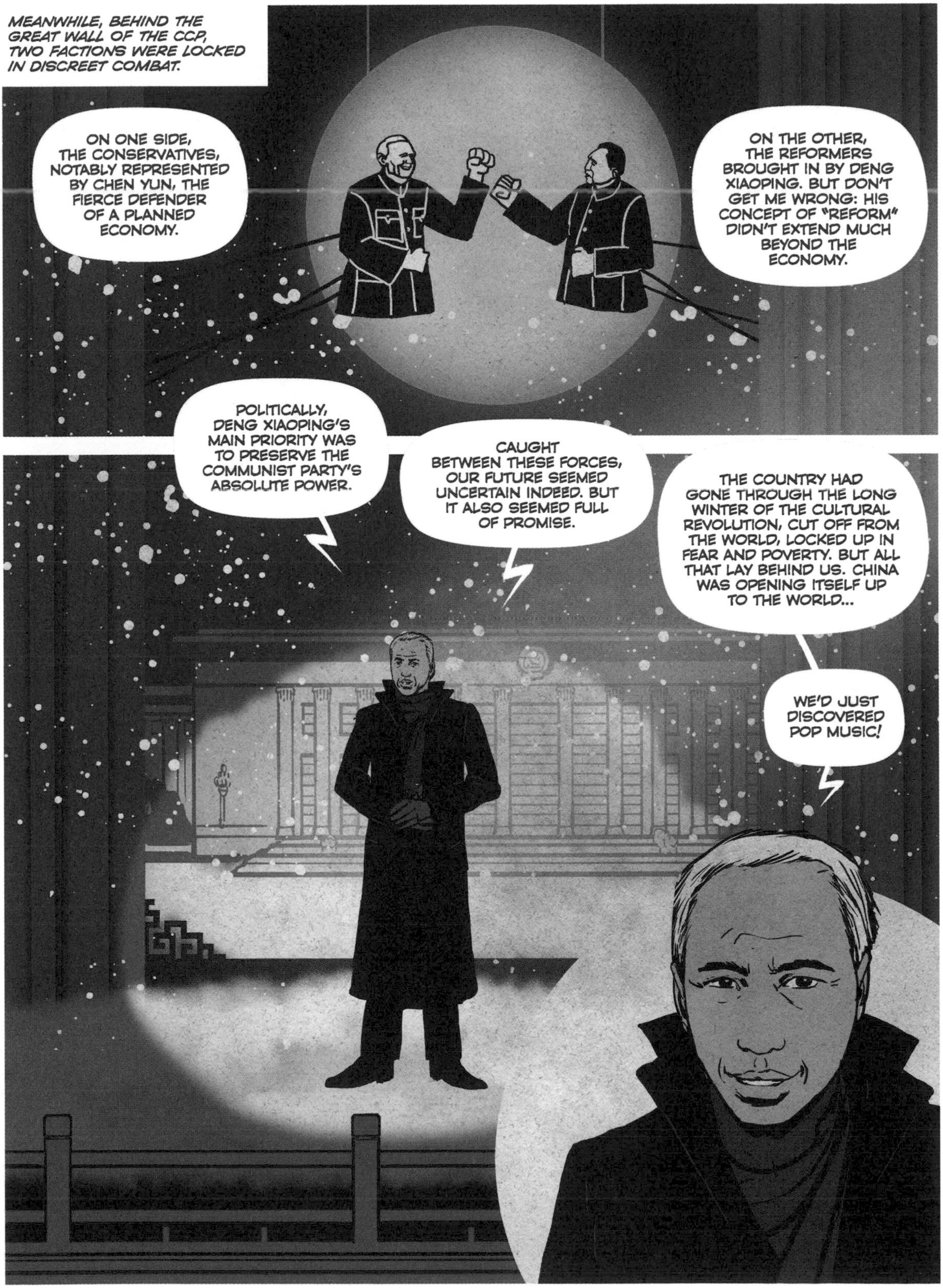
MEANWHILE, BEHIND THE GREAT WALL OF THE CCP, TWO FACTIONS WERE LOCKED IN DISCREET COMBAT.
ON ONE SIDE, THE CONSERVATIVES, NOTABLY REPRESENTED BY CHEN YUN, THE FIERCE DEFENDER OF A PLANNED ECONOMY.
ON THE OTHER, THE REFORMERS BROUGHT IN BY DENG XIAOPING. BUT DON'T GET ME WRONG: HIS CONCEPT OF "REFORM" DIDN'T EXTEND MUCH BEYOND THE ECONOMY.
POLITICALLY, DENG XIAOPING'S MAIN PRIORITY WAS TO PRESERVE THE COMMUNIST PARTY'S ABSOLUTE POWER.
CAUGHT BETWEEN THESE FORCES, OUR FUTURE SEEMED UNCERTAIN INDEED. BUT IT ALSO SEEMED FULL OF PROMISE.
THE COUNTRY HAD GONE THROUGH THE LONG WINTER OF THE CULTURAL REVOLUTION, CUT OFF FROM THE WORLD, LOCKED UP IN FEAR AND POVERTY. BUT ALL THAT LAY BEHIND US. CHINA WAS OPENING ITSELF UP TO THE WORLD...
WE'D JUST DISCOVERED POP MUSIC!

BEIJING, 1985

DON'T BOTHER LOOKING FOR ME AMONG THE 15,000 ATTENDEES AT THE WORKERS' GYMNASIUM IN BEIJING. I WASN'T THERE WITH MY COMRADES AT THE FIRST POP CONCERT IN THE HISTORY OF THE PEOPLE'S REPUBLIC.

I GLADLY MET UP WITH THEM IN THE MANY TINY BOOKSTORES POPPING UP AROUND THE UNIVERSITIES ON THE OUTSKIRTS, FAR FROM THE HEART OF THE CITY. THESE MARVELOUS HOLES-IN-THE-WALL PROVIDED SHELTER FOR THE FIRST INROADS OF WESTERN IDEAS, WHICH WE WERE JUST DISCOVERING. IN THOSE DAYS, OUR THIRST TO READ, LEARN, AND EXPLORE THE OUTSIDE WORLD WAS INSATIABLE.

DID YOU GET THAT TRANSLATION OF *BEING AND NOTHINGNESS* YET?

WE SOLD OUT ALREADY!

AND HEIDEGGER?

AND FREUD?

DOES THE UNCONSCIOUS STILL FASCINATE YOU, MISS YU?

LET ME CHECK.

MEANWHILE, HERE'S THE LATEST VOLUME FROM *TOWARDS THE FUTURE!*

IT WAS IN THIS SPIRIT OF OPENNESS THAT JIN GUANTAO AND BAO ZUNXIN FOUNDED THE IMPRINT *TOWARDS THE FUTURE* IN 1984.

TOWARDS THE FUTURE ALSO FEATURED TRANSLATIONS, INCLUDING FREUD'S *SELECTED WORKS* AND THE CLUB OF ROME'S *LIMITS TO GROWTH*.

SOME VOLUMES OF THESE PROGRESSIVE ESSAYS, LIKE *THE DIFFICULTIES OF CONFUCIANISM*, SOLD OVER A MILLION COPIES THROUGHOUT CHINA!

THE IMPRINT DID NOT SURVIVE THE SPRING OF 1989. AFTER TIANANMEN, JIN MOVED TO HONG KONG, AND BAO WAS SENTENCED TO FIVE YEARS IN PRISON.

WE HAD IMPROMPTU DEBATES AND REFERRED TO OUR MEETINGS WITH A FRENCH WORD: "SALON." SOMETIMES WE HELD SALONS IN OUR DORM ROOM.

THE THEME OF TODAY'S SALON IS "HOW CHINA'S MODERNIZATION PROCESS HAS FAILED."

OR "WHY OUR COUNTRY NEVER MANAGED TO TRANSITION TO MODERNITY IN THE 20TH CENTURY."

I'D LIKE TO BRING UP THE PROCESS OF DEMOCRATIZATION IN SOUTH KOREA, WHICH SEEMS TO BE GOING WELL!

THESE DISCUSSIONS WENT ON LATE INTO THE NIGHT, IN A VARIETY OF PLACES. BEIJING WAS A HOTBED OF IMPASSIONED DEBATES!

WHY, WE'RE CREATING CHINA'S OWN ENLIGHTENMENT!

LOOK, BO LIN!

IT'S HIM! THE FAMOUS MARADONA!

SUDDENLY, TV WAS SHOWING US IMAGES FROM ALL OVER THE WORLD.

IN OUR EYES, NO TELEVISED EVENT WAS AS IMPORTANT AS DEATHSONG OF THE RIVER.

ON JUNE 13, 1987, CREWS FROM LUOYANG AND BEIJING DRIFTED DOWN THE YELLOW RIVER.

THE CRAFT CAPSIZED IN THE LOWER LAJIA GORGE.

CAN YOU TURN IT UP?

TWO PEOPLE WERE DROWNED.

REPORTS SAY THESE YOUNG PEOPLE RISKED THEIR LIVES TO KEEP AN AMERICAN FROM BEING THE FIRST TO DESCEND THE YELLOW RIVER.

THEY SACRIFICED THEIR LIVES TO THE YELLOW RIVER. MUST THE PATRIOTISM OF THESE YOUTHS BE GLORIFIED? OR SHOULD THEIR RECKLESS SENTIMENT BE CRITICIZED?

BROADCAST IN JUNE AND AUGUST 1988, THESE SIX EPISODES QUESTIONED TRADITIONAL VALUES AND CALLED FOR THE OPENING OF CHINA.

IT WAS TIME OUR YELLOW RIVER, THE SYMBOL OF OLD CHINA, FLOWED INTO THE BLUE SEAS OF THE WORLD AND EMBRACED THE WEST.

THE SUCCESS OF THIS DOCUMENTARY SERIES MARKED THE HIGH POINT OF A PERIOD NOW CALLED "CULTURAL FEVER".

A BRIEF AND MAGNIFICENT TIME THAT WAS TO END A YEAR LATER, ON THE GRANITE OF TIANANMEN.

ON APRIL 4, 1989, EVERYTHING CHANGED.

ACT II

-THE DEATH OF HU YAOBANG-

EVEN TODAY, WORDS FAIL ME WHEN I TRY TO DESCRIBE THE FRUSTRATION, THE ANGER WE FELT THAT APRIL 15TH.

THE NEWS WAS ANNOUNCED BY XIAN AND XUE FEI, STAR ANCHORS OF THE STATE NETWORK CCTV.

THEY WERE ALSO THE ONES WHO WOULD COVER TIANANMEN SQUARE.

COMRADE HU YAOBANG HAS PASSED AWAY.

A SWORN ENEMY OF THE CONSERVATIVES, HU YAOBANG HAD ALWAYS PROTECTED INTELLECTUALS FROM PERSECUTION. ACCUSED OF ENCOURAGING THE 1986 PRO-DEMOCRACY STUDENT PROTESTS, HE HAD BEEN FORCED FROM HIS POST AS THE PARTY'S GENERAL SECRETARY. SO WE FELT SOMEHOW RESPONSIBLE FOR HIS FALL FROM GRACE.

NEVERTHELESS, HU YAOBANG REMAINED A MEMBER OF THE POLITBURO. THE NIGHT BEFORE, HE HAD STILL REPRESENTED FOR US THE POSSIBILITY OF CHANGE. WITH HIS DEATH, THAT HOPE HAD JUST BEEN SNUFFED.

NO ONE KNOWS WHO PLACED THE FIRST FLOWER AT THE FOOT OF THE MONUMENT TO THE PEOPLE'S HEROES.

BUT THEIR ACT WOULD MARK THE BEGINNING OF THE GREATEST POPULAR UPRISING IN THE HISTORY OF THE REGIME.

1) REHABILITATE HU YAOBANG AND AFFIRM HIS VIEWS ON DEMOCRACY, FREEDOM, TOLERANCE, AND SOCIAL HARMONY AS CORRECT.

2) ADMIT THAT THE CAMPAIGNS AGAINST SPIRITUAL POLLUTION AND BOURGEOIS LIBERALIZATION WERE WRONG.

3) ADOPT MEASURES AGAINST CORRUPTION AND PUBLISH INFORMATION ON THE INCOME OF STATE LEADERS AND THEIR FAMILY MEMBERS.

4) ALLOW PRIVATELY RUN NEWSPAPERS AND STOP PRESS CENSORSHIP.

5) INCREASE FUNDING FOR EDUCATION AND RAISE INTELLECTUALS' PAY.

6) END RESTRICTIONS ON DEMONSTRATIONS IN BEIJING.

7) DEMAND PUBLIC APOLOGIES FROM OUR LEADERS FOR THEIR MISTAKES AND ORGANIZE ACTUAL DEMOCRATIC ELECTIONS.

WANG DAN WAS 20 YEARS OLD, A HISTORY STUDENT AT PEKING UNIVERSITY, WHERE HE HAD FOUNDED A "SALON" ON DEMOCRACY. IN UNDER TWO YEARS, HIS NAME WOULD HEAD A LIST OF CHINA'S MOST WANTED.

THE EVENTS OF TIANANMEN TRULY BEGAN THAT DAY, WHEN HE ANNOUNCED OUR "SEVEN DEMANDS."

I THINK BACK ON THOSE SEVEN DEMANDS A LOT.

MOST OF THEM, IT SEEMS TO ME, ARE STILL VALID, AND SOONER OR LATER, CHINA WILL HAVE TO FACE THEM.

THE MOVEMENT SOON WON SUPPORT FROM PART OF THE INTELLECTUAL AND ACADEMIC ELITE.

THAT SAME DAY, A DOZEN RESPECTED FIGURES GATHERED IN THE BEIJING OFFICES OF THE WORLD ECONOMIC HERALD.

AMONG THEM WERE POLITICAL SCIENTIST YAN JIAQI, CELEBRATED INTELLECTUAL AND ACTIVIST CHEN ZIMING, AND REPORTER GE YANG. SHE HAD JOINED THE PARTY AT A VERY YOUNG AGE, BEFORE FALLING VICTIM TO AN ANTI-RIGHTIST CAMPAIGN IN THE 1960S. SHE SPENT 20 YEARS IN A FACTORY.

THESE INTELLECTUALS HAD ALL KNOWN THE PAINFUL ERA OF THE CULTURAL REVOLUTION.

IT HAD LEFT THEM FIERCELY DETERMINED TO FIGHT FOR FREEDOM AND DEMOCRACY.

NEVERTHELESS, UNLIKE THE ENTHUSIASTIC AND IDEALISTIC YOUTH, THEIR EXPERIENCE KEPT THEM CAUTIOUS WHEN IT CAME TO A REGIME WHOSE BRUTALITY THEY HAD SUFFERED FIRSTHAND.

I SEE ALL OF CHINA'S HOPES POURING INTO THE STREETS WITH THESE STUDENTS.

SOMETIMES, PRESSURE FROM THE STREETS CAN PROVE A DRIVING FORCE IN HISTORY. BUT FOR THE MOVEMENT TO ACHIEVE RESULTS, IT MUST BE COORDINATED.

IN MAY 1989, JUST AFTER HU YAOBANG'S FUNERAL, GE YANG WAS INVITED TO SPEAK AT A CONFERENCE IN THE U.S.

SHE NEVER CAME BACK.

FOR OUR FIRST MAJOR DEMONSTRATION, WE WORE THE COLORS OF MOURNING. WE WERE BUT FEW, LIKE THE SCATTERED MEMBERS OF A FAMILY REUNITED OVER THE LOSS OF A LOVED ONE. BUT UNDER THE SADNESS, ANGER WAS ALREADY BUILDING TO A ROAR.

HU YAOBANG WAS ONLY SEVENTY-THREE!

AND HOW OLD IS DENG XIAOPING?

EIGHTY-FIVE! ABROAD, YOUTH IS CONSIDERED A VIRTUE!

IN CHINA, IT'S A CURSE! THE LESS HAIR ON YOUR HEAD, THE MORE POWER YOU HAVE!

HMM... I WONDER JUST HOW THE POWERS THAT BE WILL PAY TRIBUTE TO HU YAOBANG...

BUT A FEW MILES AWAY, IN THE LIVING ROOM OF HIS RESIDENCE, PATRIARCH DENG ZIAOPING HAD NO IDEA OF THE WAVE THAT WAS ABOUT TO BREAK OVER BEIJING.

TRUTH BE TOLD, I MYSELF COULD NEVER HAVE PREDICTED THE SCOPE THAT THE MOVEMENT WOULD TAKE IN THE DAYS TO COME.

DAY 4. WEDNESDAY, APRIL 19.

LIU GANG AND I WENT WAY BACK. WE'D MET AT PEKING UNIVERSITY IN THE '80S. HE'D BEEN A BRILLIANT SCIENCE STUDENT. THEN HE'D QUIT HIS JOB AS AN ENGINEER TO BECOME A POLITICAL ACTIVIST. SINCE THEN, HE'D ROAMED FROM CAMPUS TO CAMPUS, PROMOTING DEMOCRACY, CRASHING WITH ONE FRIEND AND THEN ANOTHER. WHEN HE CAME TO BEIJING, I PUT HIM UP. HE GATHERED MANY STUDENTS AROUND HIM THAT WOULD END UP IN TIANANMEN SQUARE.

YOU BETTER RUN. YOU CAN'T LET THE POLICE SEE YOU HERE.

SHOW YOURSELF, LI PENG!

SHOW YOURSELF, LI PENG!

WU'ER KAIXI, ON THE OTHER HAND—I WAS SEEING HIM FOR THE FIRST TIME. HE WAS 21, A STUDENT AT BEIJING NORMAL UNIVERSITY. HE HAD A GIFT FOR CAPTIVATING CROWDS. WE'D MEET AGAIN.

WHAT DO WE DEMAND? HU YAOBANG'S IMMEDIATE REHABILITATION!

MEANWHILE, TO NO ONE'S SURPRISE, THE EVENING ENDED IN A HAIL OF
BILLY CLUBS. BUT IT'D TAKE A LOT MORE THAN THAT TO DISCOURAGE US.

<BUXU
DA REN!*>

*YOU'RE NOT ALLOWED TO HIT US!

<BUXU DA
REN!!!*>

AND SO, THAT APRIL, THE
PIECES WERE LAID OUT ONE
BY ONE ON THE CHESSBOARD
OF TIANANMEN.

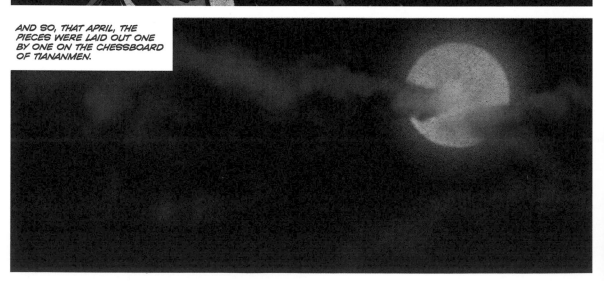

DAY 7. SATURDAY, APRIL 22.

AFTER OUR FIRST NIGHT OUT ON THE SQUARE, DAWN'S EARLY LIGHT AFFORDED LITTLE WARMTH.

SUDDENLY, ALL TIANANMEN WAS ON ITS FEET BEFORE THE BANNERS OF THE PEOPLE'S REPUBLIC OF CHINA. THERE WERE 100,000 OF US, AND WE WERE ALL PATRIOTS.

THE DAY WENT ON. WE DIDN'T MOVE. WE MADE NO DEMANDS. WE SIMPLY WISHED TO PAY TRIBUTE TO HU YAOBANG.

THAT MOMENT MARKED ME, JUST AS IT MARKED EVERYONE WHO LIVED THROUGH THAT SPRING. BEHIND THE WALLS OF THE GREAT HALL OF THE PEOPLE, 4,000 HIGH OFFICIALS WERE TAKING PART IN HU YAOBANG'S FUNERAL. ON THE STEPS, A DELEGATION OF STUDENTS ASKED TO SEE PRIME MINISTER LI PENG, TO RECEIVE MORE OBJECTIVE COVERAGE FROM THE MEDIA, AND TO BE ALLOWED A MOMENT OF REFLECTION BEFORE HU YAOBANG'S REMAINS.

AS THEY DID SO, THEY MADE THE TRADITIONAL GESTURE OF SUBJECTS REQUESTING AN AUDIENCE FROM THE EMPEROR: KNEELING, HANDS RAISED HEAVENWARD, BRANDISHING THEIR LETTERS OF GRIEVANCE.

THEY WAITED IN THE SUN UNTIL THEIR KNEES HURT. IN VAIN. THE PEOPLE COULD NOT ENTER THE GREAT HALL OF THE PEOPLE. THE POWERS THAT BE TURNED A DEAF EAR.

IN THE END, HU YAOBANG'S BODY WAS SMUGGLED OUT THROUGH A HIDDEN DOOR.

THEY HAD NOT GRANTED US THE RIGHT TO SAY OUR GOODBYES.

WE HEADED BACK TO OUR UNIVERSITIES, EXHAUSTED BY THE SLEEPLESS NIGHT AND A DAY OF GRIEVING, WHEN SUDDENLY, WE FOUND SOLDIERS IN FORMATION AWAITING US AT THE END OF THE AVENUE. WE'D WANTED A DIALOGUE, AND OUR LEADERS HAD DISPATCHED THE ARMY. THE PRESENCE OF THESE TROOPS, FAR FROM THREATENING, SENT US A MESSAGE. THIS WAS DENG XIAOPING'S ANSWER.

LOOK!

WE WEREN'T AFRAID. QUITE THE OPPOSITE. THESE SOLDIERS MERELY FANNED THE FLAMES OF OUR WRATH. THE NEXT DAY, STUDENTS AND PROFESSORS WENT ON STRIKE.

CLASSES BECAME MEETINGS. CAMPUSES THRUMMED WITH A THOUSAND DEBATES. THE MOVEMENT WAS GROWING INEXORABLY, SPREADING THROUGHOUT ALL CHINA FROM XI'AN TO SHANGHAI, WUHAN TO CHENGSOU. STUDENTS WERE MOBILIZING.

HOW LONG WOULD IT LAST?

NO ONE COULD SAY.

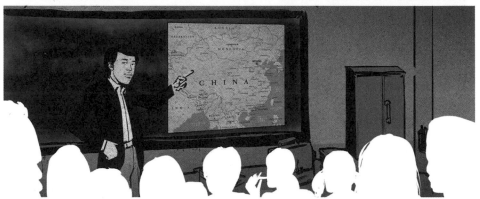

HEARD THE NEWS? XU GOT HER SCHOLARSHIP AND HER VISA!

WHAT LUCK! THAT'S WONDERFUL!

YES. SHE'LL BE LEAVING BEFORE THE SUMMER'S OVER... IF ALL GOES WELL.

WE WERE ALL MOVING FORWARD WITH OUR PLANS FOR THE FUTURE. SHILIN WAS ESPECIALLY INTERESTED IN THE NEXT VOLLEYBALL CHAMPIONSHIP. LILI STILL WANTED TO BE A PROFESSOR. AS FOR XU, WHO WAS FROM DANDONG NEAR THE KOREAN BORDER—ALL SHE DREAMED ABOUT WAS BERLIN. SHE WAS THE ONLY PERSON IN BEIJING WHO KNEW THE GERMAN SINGER NENA'S LYRICS BY HEART.

99 LUFTBALLONS. AUF IHREM WEG ZUM HORIZONT...

IT WAS AN EDITORIAL THAT SET OUR MOVEMENT DOWN A PATH OF NO RETURN.

TO UNDERSTAND WHAT HAPPENED NEXT, YOU HAVE TO KNOW THAT *THE PEOPLE'S DAILY* WAS NO ORDINARY NEWSPAPER.

THE *PEOPLE'S DAILY* WAS THE PARTY'S PRESS ORGAN. THE OPINIONS THEREIN DID NOT BELONG TO JOURNALISTS, BUT TO NO LESS THAN THE MEN IN CHARGE.

AT THE TIME, IT HAD A PRINT RUN OF OVER FIVE MILLION COPIES. ITS PAGES WERE PUT UP IN THE STREETS. ITS EDITORIALS WERE BROADCAST ON NATIONAL RADIO.

HERE IS WHAT THE CHINESE PEOPLE HEARD AT 8PM ON APRIL 25, 1989, AND WHAT THEY WOULD READ THE NEXT DAY IN THE PAPER:

"...ABNORMAL PHENOMENA HAVE ALSO OCCURRED DURING THE MOURNING ACTIVITIES. TAKING ADVANTAGE OF THE SITUATION, AN EXTREMELY SMALL NUMBER OF PEOPLE SPREAD RUMORS, ATTACKED PARTY AND STATE LEADERS BY NAME, AND INSTIGATED THE MASSES TO BREAK INTO THE XINHUA GATE AT ZHONGNANHAI, WHERE THE PARTY CENTRAL COMMITTEE AND THE STATE COUNCIL ARE LOCATED.

"SOME PEOPLE EVEN SHOUTED SUCH REACTIONARY SLOGANS AS, 'DOWN WITH THE COMMUNIST PARTY.'"

...THEY VILIFIED, HURLED INVECTIVES AT, AND ATTACKED PARTY AND STATE LEADERS. BLATANTLY VIOLATING THE CONSTITUTION, THEY CALLED FOR OPPOSITION TO THE LEADERSHIP OF THE COMMUNIST PARTY AND THE SOCIALIST SYSTEM.

AFTER THE MEMORIAL MEETING, A SMALL NUMBER OF PEOPLE WITH ULTERIOR PURPOSES CONTINUED TO TAKE ADVANTAGE OF THE STUDENTS' FEELINGS OF GRIEF FOR COMRADE HU YAOBANG AND SPREAD RUMORS TO POISON PEOPLE'S MINDS...

...THEIR PURPOSE WAS TO SOW DISSENSION AMONG THE PEOPLE, PLUNGE THE WHOLE COUNTRY INTO CHAOS AND SABOTAGE THE POLITICAL SITUATION OF STABILITY AND UNITY.

IN THE NATIONAL RADIO ANNOUNCER, WE HEARD THE VOICE OF DENG XIAOPING. IF THAT VICIOUS AND UNNUANCED EDITORICAL WAS HIS RESPONSE, SO BE IT.

WE WOULD RETURN TO TIANANMEN!

I REMEMBER THAT MORNING: POLLEN DRIFTING ON THE COOL AIR.

SPRINGTIME WAS HERE. SPRING, 1989.

DAY 12. THURSDAY, APRIL 27.

THERE WERE MANY OF US—MANY, MANY OF US—CONVERGING ON TIANANMEN FROM EVERY UNIVERSITY THAT DAY.

WE KNEW THAT SOMETHING BIG WAS HAPPENING, SOMETHING IMPORTANT AND UNIQUE. DOWN THE STREETS AND THE AVENUES WE CAME, ADVANCING BY THE THOUSANDS, TENS OF THOUSANDS. OUR RANKS SWELLED, OUR STRENGTH GREW. SO DID OUR RESOLVE.

WE CAME UP AGAINST THE FIRST ROADBLOCK. FOR A MOMENT, THE POLICEMEN STARED US DOWN.

THEN THEY GAVE WAY.

IN THE FACE OF THAT HUMAN TIDE, THEY STEPPED ASIDE. WE PASSED THROUGH EVERY ROADBLOCK, ONE BY ONE, STREET AFTER STREET.

THERE WERE 100,000 OF US MARCHING WHEN WE REACHED TIANANMEN.

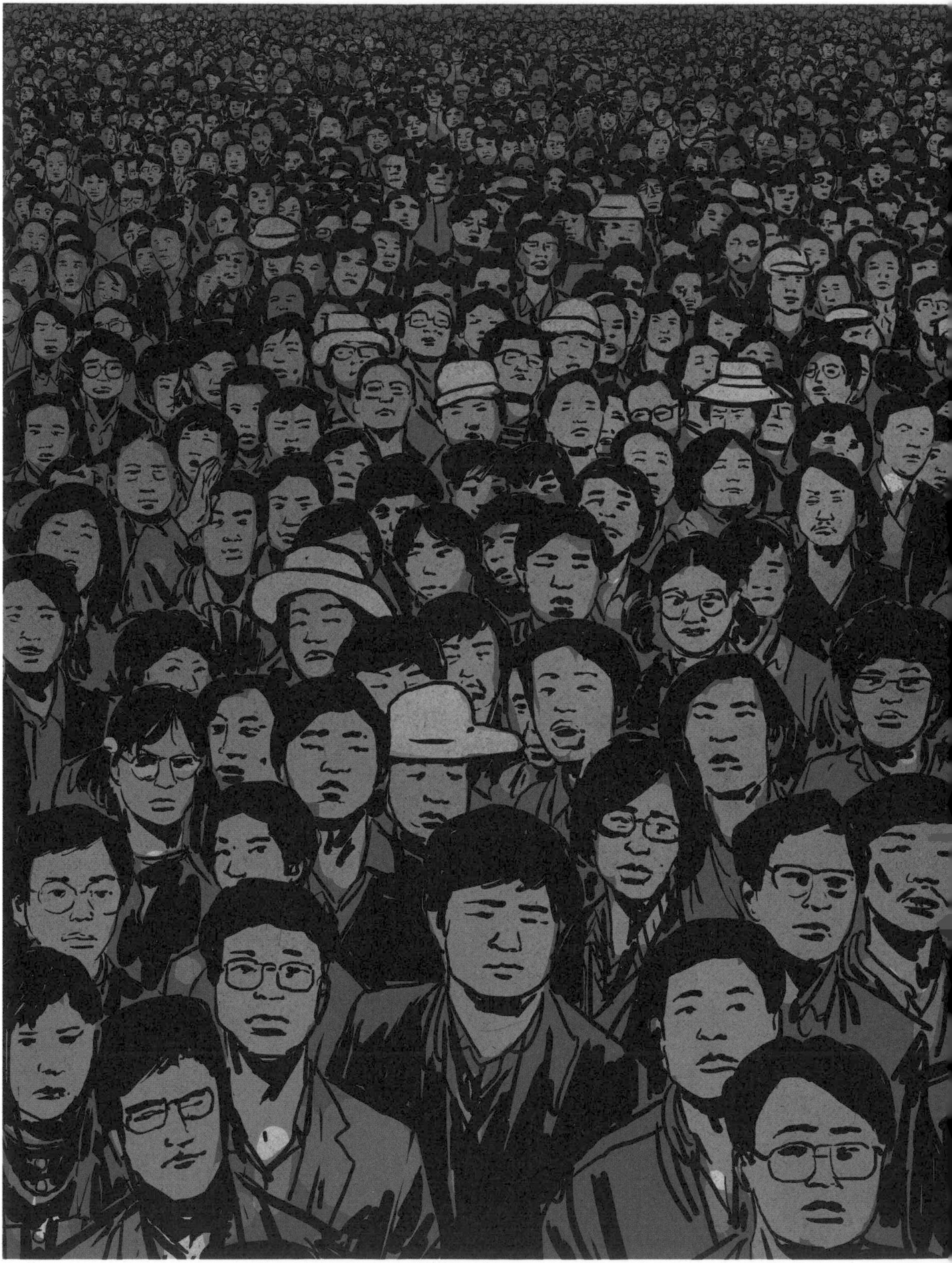

WHERE WE JOINED A GROUP MORE THAN A MILLION STRONG!

NO ONE HAD BEEN SUMMONED. THE LARGEST SPONTANEOUS GATHERING IN ALL OF CHINESE HISTORY NOW SURROUNDED TIANANMEN SQUARE!

THE HEAVY ATMOSPHERE OF MOURNING HAD LIFTED. ALL AROUND ME NOW WAS NOTHING BUT THE JOY AND SMILES OF BEIJING'S YOUTH.

YOU MUST BE STARVING.

HERE, EAT UP. GO AHEAD— IT'S ON THE HOUSE!

BY THE END OF DAY, WE WERE ELATED AND EXHAUSTED, WITH SEVERAL MORE MILES OF MARCHING TO GO BEFORE WE REACHED OUR UNIVERSITIES ON THE CAPITAL'S OUTSKIRTS. ALL ALONG THE WAY, THE PEOPLE OF BEIJING GAVE US WATER, FRUIT, STEAMED BUNS—EVEN MONEY. I KNEW THAT THEY SUPPORTED OUR CAUSE. LIKE US, THEY WANTED CHINA TO CHANGE. WE WERE SPEAKING FOR THEM AS WELL.

WE ARE THE SONS OF THE PEOPLE!

FROM THAT DAY—APRIL 27—ONWARD, WE DEMANDED THE PARTY RECOGNIZE THE LEGITIMACY OF OUR MOVEMENT. IT WASN'T ABOUT "TRIBUTE" ANYMORE: IT WAS ABOUT FREEDOM AND DEMOCRACY.

TO OLD DENG, WHO HAD BEGUN AND BEEN THE VICTIM OF SO MANY CAMPAIGNS OF REPRESSION, THE SITUATION WAS AT ONCE INCOMPREHENSIBLE AND HUMILIATING. HE HAD COUNTED ON THE VITRIOL OF THE EDITORIAL IN THE *PEOPLE'S DAILY* TO INSTILL A CLIMATE OF TERROR THAT WOULD SEND THE STUDENTS BACK TO THEIR UNIVERSITIES.

INSTEAD, THE STUDENTS HAD RESPONDED... WITH A MARCH!

SURPRISED BY THE UNPRECEDENTED RESPONSE, THE PARTY ATTEMPTED... UNPRECEDENTED MEASURES.

ON APRIL 29, FOR THE FIRST TIME IN CHINA'S HISTORY, A DELEGATION OF STUDENTS SPOKE WITH A HIGH PARTY CADRE LIVE ON TV.

AS OUR PARTY LEADER SAYS...

AS OUR PARTY LEADER SAYS...

AS OUR PARTY LEADER SAYS...

NO, IT'S VERY MODERN, I SWEAR! WHEN AMERICAN CHILDREN GET CRANKY, THEIR PARENTS SIT THEM DOWN RIGHT IN FRONT OF THE TV!

THIS DISCUSSION WENT NOWHERE. WE HOPED TO MEET WITH SOMEONE WHO MATTERED, BUT THE PARTY SENT YUAN MU, A MINION TOO DULL TO THINK FOR HIMSELF.

AS OUR PARTY LEADER SAYS...

HIS ONLY IDEA HAD BEEN NOT WEARING A TIE, TO LOOK "YOUNG." WHAT A JOKE.

STILL, THE STATE MEDIA WAS EVOLVING...

DAY 19. THURSDAY, MAY 4.

ALL AROUND TIANANMEN, JOURNALISTS WERE DEMANDING GREATER FREEDOM WITH THE BANNER: "DON'T FORCE US TO TELL LIES!"

A FEW DAYS EARLIER IN SHANGHAI, THE PARTY HAD SHUT DOWN THE WORLD ECONOMIC HERALD, WHICH HAD MADE THE MISTAKE OF GIVING AN HONEST ACCOUNT OF THE STUDENT PROTESTS.

MEANWHILE, WE WENT BACK TO TIANANMEN TO CELEBRATE THE ANNIVERSARY OF THE MAY FOURTH MOVEMENT.

WE WERE THE CHILDREN OF THOSE HEROES WHO HAD PROTESTED HERE SEVENTY YEARS AGO WHEN THE TREATY OF VERSAILLES CEDED SHANDONG, THE GERMAN CONCESSION, TO THE JAPANESE EMPIRE. LIKE OUR ANCESTORS, WE FELT ANGRY AND HUMILIATED. LIKE THEM, WE WERE PROTESTING FOR OUR COUNTRY'S INDEPENDENCE, FOR FREEDOM AND DEMOCRACY. LIKE THEM, WE COULD SAY, "THE CHINESE PEOPLE CAN BE KILLED BUT WE WILL NEVER SURRENDER." WE, TOO, WERE NOW PART OF CHINA'S GREAT HISTORY.

TO DISPEL A MISCONCEPTION: THE EVENTS I'M RECOUNTING ARE USUALLY PORTRAYED AS A HEAD-ON COLLISION BETWEEN STUDENTS AND THE RULING POWERS. BUT WE DIDN'T NECESSARILY SEE OURSELVES AS THEIR ADVERSARIES. DENG XIAOPING HAD INITIATED ECONOMIC REFORMS. WE MERELY FOUND IT LOGICAL TO EXTEND THESE REFORMS INTO SOCIAL AND POLITICAL REALMS.

BUT WE SOON REALIZED THAT SOMEONE BEHIND THE WALLS OF THE GREAT HALL OF THE PEOPLE HAD HEARD OUR CRY. ON MAY 4TH, DURING A HIGH LEVEL OFFICIAL MEETING, THE PARTY'S GENERAL SECRETARY, ZHAO ZIYANG, ATTEMPTED A DELICATE POLITICAL MANEUVER.

I AM SURE THERE WILL BE NO SERIOUS TROUBLE. WE MUST RESPOND TO THE STUDENTS' REASONABLE REQUESTS WITH LAWFUL AND DEMOCRATIC MEANS.

NOW WE KNEW THAT FAR ABOVE US, IN THE HIGHEST SPHERES OF THE PARTY, TWO FACTIONS WITH DIVERGENT OPINIONS WERE AT LOGGERHEADS.

REFORMERS LIKE ZHAO ZIYANG WERE WILLING TO HEAR US OUT, TO BE OPEN AND ACCOMMODATING. BUT ACROSS THE AISLE, THE CONSERVATIVES LED BY PRIME MINISTER LI PENG, SAW THINGS OTHERWISE.

EACH SIDE TOOK TURNS MOVING PIECES ABOUT THE BOARD. ONLY ONE VICTOR WOULD EMERGE.

WHEN THE GAME WAS OVER, WOULD DENG XIAOPING DECLARE HIMSELF FOR RED OR BLACK?

MEANWHILE, I MARCHED WITH THE OTHER STUDENTS. THEY SEEMED CHEERFUL, CAREFREE... AND MOST OF ALL, SO YOUNG! HOW OLD COULD THEY HAVE BEEN? 18? 20? 22 AT THE MOST? THEIR TEENAGE YEARS HAD JUST ENDED. THEIR PASTS WERE NO BURDEN. I UNDERSTOOD THEM, AND YET I WAS AWARE OF A DISTANCE BETWEEN US. UNLIKE THEM, BY AGE 26, I'D LIVED THROUGH THE REGIME'S MOST VIOLENT YEARS. SO WHEN I HEARD THEM SINGING, DEBATING, DISCUSSING THE FUTURE AND GETTING EXCITED, I FELT A NAMELESS ANXIETY GROWING INSIDE ME...

EARLY MAY WAS SUNNY AND MILD. AND AT LEAST ONE THING WAS REASSURING. ZHAO ZIYANG'S CONCILIATORY REMARKS HAD BROUGHT STUDENTS BACK TO THEIR CLASSROOMS. I COULDN'T TELL WHAT THE NEXT STEP FOR THEIR MOVEMENT MIGHT BE.

THEY WERE SO TIRED. AND YET...

PSSH!!

C'MON, EVERYONE! GLASSES!

GAN BEI!

BOTTOMS UP! GAN BEI!

GAN BEI!

SO... DO WE STOP HERE?

YESTERDAY, A MILLION PEOPLE IN TIANANMEN SQUARE, AND TOMORROW—BACK TO SCHOOL! LIKE NOTHING HAPPENED. I CAN'T BELIEVE IT!

PSSHH!!

WE MUST KEEP UP THE PRESSURE! WE MUST—

A HUNGER STRIKE!

JUST LIKE GANDHI!

I DON'T KNOW IF THEY'D REALLY READ GANDHI, BUT THAT'S HOW THE HUNGER STRIKE BEGAN.

ACT III
-THE HUNGER STRIKE-

不是动乱
This is not "turmoil"

立刻对话，不许推诿
Dialogue now! No more dawdling!

外国媒体，请支持我们！
World press, please support us!

国际舆论，请帮助我们！
International public opinion, please come to our aid!

民主的力量，加入我们！
Democratic forces, please stand by us!

为人民绝食，我们别无选择！
Fasting for the people! We have no choice!

立即平反
Yes to rehabilitation right now!

MANIFESTO FOR A HUNGER STRIKE

DEAR COUNTRYMEN, FOLLOWING UP ON OUR MOMENTOUS DEMONSTRATIONS, TODAY WE RESOLVE TO BEGIN A HUNGER STRIKE IN TIANANMEN SQUARE.

OUR REASONS ARE:

1) TO PROTEST THE GOVERNMENT'S INDIFFERENCE TOWARD OUR BOYCOTT OF CLASSES

2) TO PROTEST THE GOVERNMENT'S LABELING OUR PATRIOTIC, DEMOCRATIC STUDENT MOVEMENT AS "TURMOIL;" AND MANY DISTORTED PRESS REPORTS

WE DEMAND OF THE GOVERNMENT:

1) IMMEDIATE DIALOGUE—CONCRETE, SUBSTANTIVE, AND ON EQUAL TERMS—WITH THE DIALOGUE DELEGATION OF BEIJING COLLEGE STUDENTS.

2) A FAIR AND UNBIASED ACKNOWLEDGMENT OF THE LEGITIMACY OF THE STUDENT MOVEMENT, LABELING IT "PATRIOTIC" AND "DEMOCRATIC"

TIME FOR COMMENCEMENT OF THE HUNGER STRIKE: 2:00 P.M., MAY 13.

PLACE OF THE HUNGER STRIKE: TIANANMEN SQUARE

UNTIL NOW, A MASS HUNGER STRIKE HAD NEVER BEEN USED AS POLITICAL LEVERAGE IN CHINA.

FOR THE STUDENTS, IT WAS A CLEVER WAY TO INTENSIFY PRESSURE ON THE GOVERNMENT WHILE REMAINING PEACEFUL.

THEY WOULD NOT RESORT TO VIOLENCE. INSTEAD, THEY WOULD TURN IT ON THEMSELVES.

THIS PIVOTAL DECISION CAME OUT OF THE BLUE, BUT ITS DEPLOYMENT WAS ORGANIZED WITH ASTONISHING EFFICIENCY.

LISTS WERE PASSED AROUND. VOLUNTEERS SIGNED UP. OUTFITS WERE IMPROVISED.

THE CAFETERIA AT PEKING UNIVERSITY EVEN SERVED A SYMBOLIC "LAST SUPPER" FOR THE HUNGER STRIKERS.

AND THE MOVEMENT TOOK ON A NEW SCOPE.

MORE RADICAL, MORE TRAGIC... MORE DANGEROUS, TOO.

DAY 28. SATURDAY, MAY 13.

THE HUNGER STRIKE MEANT PERMANENTLY OCCUPYING THE SQUARE.

THERE WERE ABOUT 2,000 STUDENTS DETERMINED TO LIE THERE AND NOT MOVE.

AFTER A DAY, A LIGHT HAD ALREADY FADED FROM THEIR EYES.

ALL AROUND THEM, THE SQUARE BECAME A PLACE TO LIVE THAT I WOULD HELP ORGANIZE.

NEW FIGURES EMERGED, SUCH AS CHAI LING, WHOM THE WESTERN PRESS NICKNAMED THE "PASIONARA OF TIANANMEN."

A PSYCHOLOGY STUDENT AT BEIJING NORMAL UNIVERSITY, CHAI LING CAME TO LEAD THE GROUP OF HUNGER STRIKERS.

ONCE A MODEL MEMBER OF THE COMMUNIST YOUTH LEAGUE OF CHINA, AT AGE 22 SHE HAD AN OBVIOUS FLAIR FOR WIELDING A MEGAPHONE.

IN THIS BRIGHT, SUNNY MONTH OF MAY, WE HAVE BEGUN A HUNGER STRIKE.

DURING THE GLORIOUS DAYS OF OUR YOUTH, WE DO NOT DESIRE TO ABANDON THE BEAUTY OF LIFE. YET WE HAVE NO OTHER CHOICE!

DO NOT FEEL SORRY FOR US, MOTHERS AND FATHERS, AS WE SUFFER FROM HUNGER. DO NOT FEEL SAD, UNCLES AND AUNTS, WHEN WE BID FAREWELL TO LIFE. OUR ONLY DESIRE IS THAT THE CHINESE PEOPLE ENJOY BETTER LIVES. WE HAVE BUT ONE REQUEST: PLEASE DO NOT FORGET THAT WE DID NOT SEEK DEATH.

DEMOCRACY IS NOT THE CONCERN OF ONLY A FEW, AND THE BUILDING OF DEMOCRACY CANNOT BE ACCOMPLISHED IN A SINGLE GENERATION.

I REMEMBER CLIMBING UP THE MONUMENT TO THE PEOPLE'S HEROES THAT AFTERNOON BESIDE A STUDENT LEADER, SHAO JING.

中央美院敬

THE CROWDS IN TIANANMEN SQUARE STRETCHED ALL AROUND ME, AS FAR AS THE EYE COULD SEE. TIANANMEN HAD BECOME A VERITABLE CITY WHERE HUNDREDS OF THOUSANDS OF STUDENTS AND ONLOOKERS HAD GATHERED. BUT ONE THING SURPRISED ME...

THE FORCES OF LAW AND ORDER HAD VANISHED! I COULDN'T MAKE OUT A SINGLE SOLDIER'S CAP OR THE HINT OF A UNIFORM AMIDST THIS SEA OF PEOPLE. THE ARMY AND THE POLICE HAD DESERTED TIANANMEN!

SUDDENLY, THE PARTY'S STRATEGY SEEMED CLEAR. THE ARMY WAS STILL NEARBY, WAITING FOR THE FIRST SPARK OF VIOLENCE. IF WE GAVE THEM THE SLIGHTEST REASON TO INTERVENE, THEY WOULD BRUTALLY CLEAR US OUT. FOR THE MOVEMENT TO LAST, WE NEEDED COHERENT ORGANIZATION. I WOULD HELP PROVIDE THAT IN THE WEEKS THAT FOLLOWED.

FROM THAT MOMENT ON, I NEVER SLEPT.

WE DIVIDED THE SQUARE INTO SEVERAL AREAS, AND PUT TWO LINES BETWEEN US AND THE POLICE. ONE SURROUNDED TIANANMEN, AND THE OTHER THE MONUMENT TO THE PEOPLE'S HEROES. WE SET SPACE ASIDE FOR AN INFIRMARY, PROTECTED THE HUNGER STRIKERS, AND MAINTAINED AN ACCESS CORRIDOR FOR AMBULANCES.

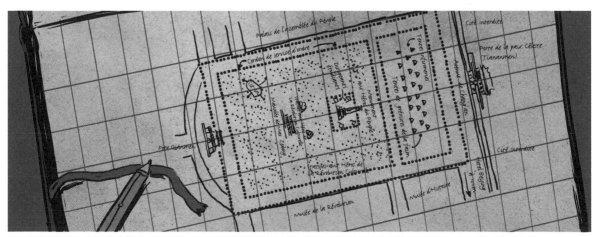

BY OCCUPYING TIANANMEN, WE HAD DEALT A TERRIBLE BLOW TO DENG XIAOPING'S PRIDE. THAT'S BECAUSE MIKHAIL GORBACHEV WAS ABOUT TO PAY HIM A VISIT...

ALLOW ME TO SUM UP A HIGHLY COMPLICATED HISTORY IN A FEW QUICK SCENES.

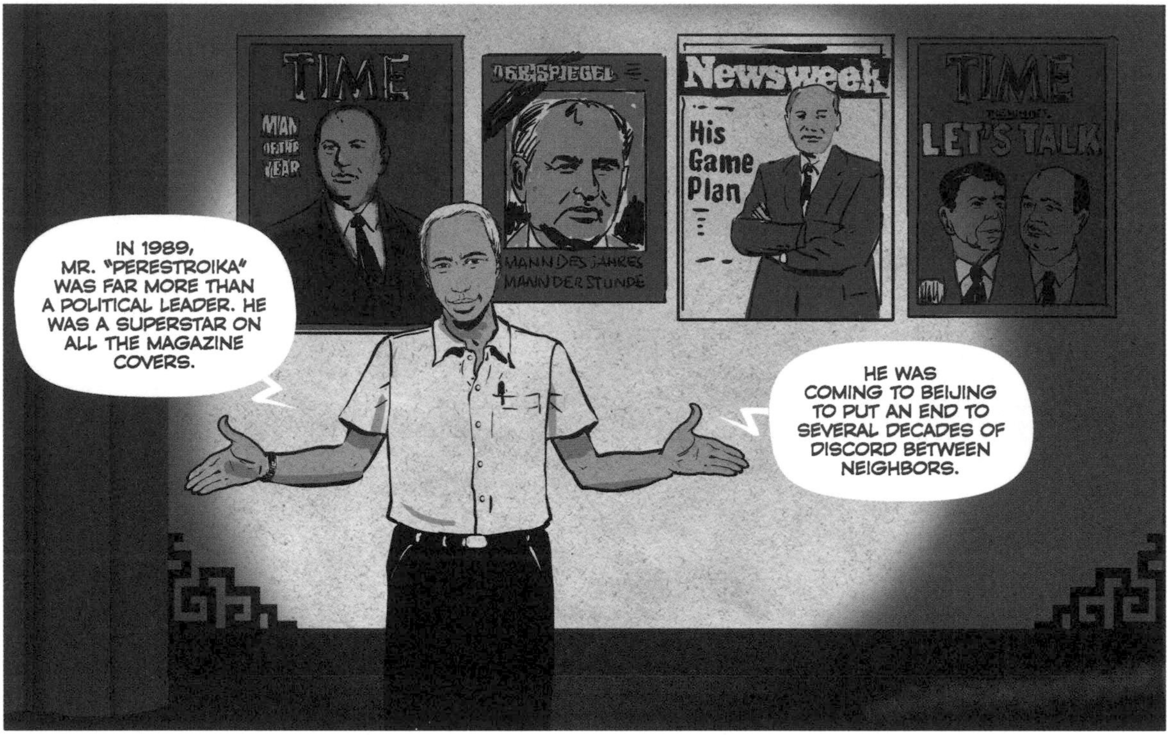
TIME
MAN OF THE YEAR
DER SPIEGEL
MANN DES JAHRES MANN DER STUNDE
Newsweek
His Game Plan
TIME
LET'S TALK
IN 1989, MR. "PERESTROIKA" WAS FAR MORE THAN A POLITICAL LEADER. HE WAS A SUPERSTAR ON ALL THE MAGAZINE COVERS.
HE WAS COMING TO BEIJING TO PUT AN END TO SEVERAL DECADES OF DISCORD BETWEEN NEIGHBORS.

IN 1950, JUST AFTER THE PEOPLE'S REPUBLIC WAS FORMED, CHINA HAD SIGNED A PACT WITH THE USSR. THE TWO GREAT COMMUNIST POWERS HAD SWORN FRIENDSHIP AND MUTUAL ASSISTANCE FOR ALL TIME.

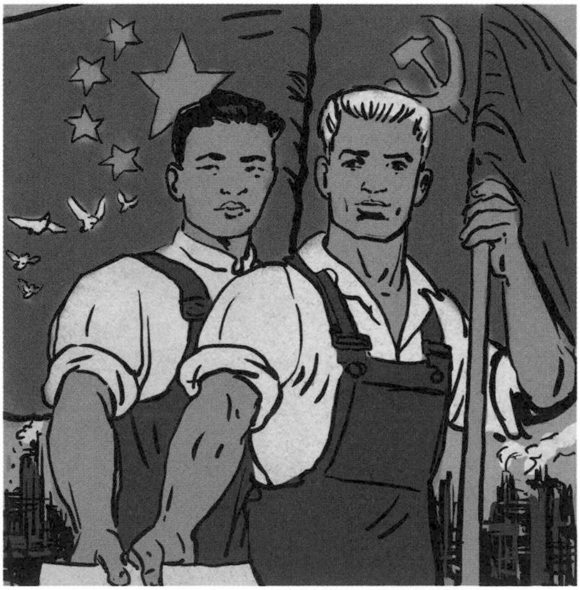

BUT JUST A DECADE LATER, THE TWO EMPIRES HAD GROWN WARY. IN 1969, THERE WAS EVEN A BRIEF BORDER SKIRMISH ALONG THE USSURI RIVER.

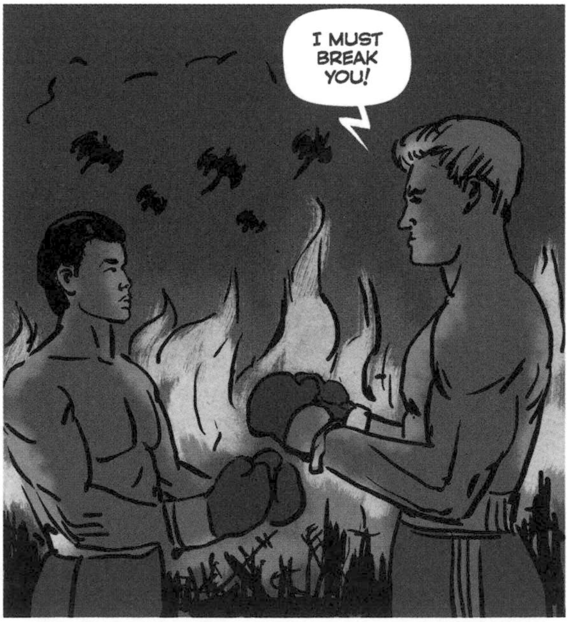
I MUST BREAK YOU!

TWENTY YEARS LATER, THE RUSSIAN LEADER'S VISIT AND THE OFFICIAL RE-ESTABLISHMENT OF RELATIONS BETWEEN THE TWO COUNTRIES SHOULD HAVE CROWNED DENG XIAOPING'S DIPLOMATIC CAREER. NO DOUBT HE DREAMT OF A PHOTO OP WITH HIS GUEST IN FRONT OF THE FORBIDDEN CITY.

BUT THERE WERE NO SCHOOLCHILDREN READY TO SING ANTHEMS IN TIANANMEN.

JUST A VAST GATHERING OF HAIRY, ANGRY STUDENTS AND HUNGER STRIKERS GROWING EVER MORE FEEBLE AND HAGGARD BENEATH A BURNING SUN.

DURING HIS VISIT, MIKHAIL GORBACHEV WAS TACTFULLY STEERED AROUND THIS SPECTACLE. BUT THE WHOLE WORLD'S EYES WERE UPON US. TO CELEBRATE THE RECONCILIATION OF CHINA AND THE USSR, THE GOVERNMENT HAD INVITED 600 JOURNALISTS FROM ALL OVER.

EVEN THE BIGGEST STARS OF AMERICAN TV HAD MADE THE TRIP, AND THE THEN-BUDDING NEWS CHANNEL CNN WAS BROADCASTING LIVE FROM BEIJING NONSTOP.

IT WAS A FACT: CHINA HAD NEVER SEEN SO MANY CAMERAS AND MICROPHONES!

WELL, WELL! MS. STEPHANIE ANDREWS OF THE BBC!

STILL WEARING MR. ANDREWS' SHIRT, I SEE!

HEY, MITCH! HOW'VE YOU BEEN SINCE TBILISI?

WE WELCOME YOU TO THE BEIJING HOTEL

THE WAY THINGS ARE, I BET WE'LL BE IN BEIJING LONGER THAN GORBACHEV!

WE MIGHT EVEN BE HERE LONGER THAN DENG XIAOPING!

58

THE PARTY WAS COUNTING ON THE FOREIGN PRESS TO IMMORTALIZE THE MEETING BETWEEN DENG AND GORBACHEV. BUT INSTEAD, THEY BROADCAST THE STUDENT OCCUPATION OF TIANANMEN LIVE, POPULARIZING A SYMPATHETIC, MODERN, AND ENDEARING IMAGE OF THEM. AND THE WHOLE WORLD ECHOED THEIR ANGER.

OVERNIGHT, THE SOVIET LEADER BECAME THE IDOL OF TIANANMEN. THE STUDENTS DIDN'T HAVE A VERY KEEN UNDERSTANDING OF HIS POLITICS, BUT CELEBRATING GORBACHEV SEEMED A GOOD WAY TO DENOUNCE DENG. ON ONE SIDE, THE SMILING PROPONENT OF GLASNOST. ON THE OTHER, THE SHRIVELED VETERAN OF THE REVOLUTION, DEAF TO THE APPEALS OF HIS OWN COUNTRY'S YOUTH.

GORBACHEV AND HIS WIFE ENTERED THE GREAT HALL OF THE PEOPLE IN SECRET, THROUGH A BACK DOOR. IN THIS HISTORIC PHOTO, DENG LOOKS LIKE AN OLD MAN CELEBRATING HIS BIRTHDAY IN A RESTAURANT WITH HIS KIDS.

YEARS LATER, DENG'S SON WOULD SHARE THIS SECRET: "MY FATHER ALWAYS CONSIDERED GORBACHEV AN IMBECILE."

BUT THE CHINESE PEOPLE WOULD REMEMBER THE VISIT DIFFERENTLY. A FEW SECONDS, CAUGHT BY AN INSOLENT CAMERAMAN.

FROM NORTH TO SOUTH, EAST TO WEST, THE FAR-FLUNG CORNERS OF THE COUNTRY, EVERYONE WAS WATCHING, RIVETED. THE PORTRAIT OF A DODDERING LEADER, UNABLE TO GET A GRIP ON HIS CHOPSTICKS DURING A STATE DINNER. THREE WEEKS EARLIER, NO ONE WOULD HAVE DARED BROADCAST FOOTAGE LIKE THAT.

IN UNDER A MONTH, THE GREAT MACHINERY OF THE STATE HAD GONE ON THE FRITZ. THE CENSORSHIP MECHANISMS WERE MALFUNCTIONING. AND AS GORBACHEV HEADED BACK TO MOSCOW IN EMBARRASSMENT, WE COULD FEEL CRACKS SPREADING THROUGH THE FOUNDATIONS OF POWER BENEATH THE FLAGSTONES OF THE SQUARE.

OF THOSE WEEKS, I RETAIN NOT ONLY MANY IMAGES, BUT ALSO SOME VERY CLEAR SOUNDS.
DAY AND NIGHT, THE CAPITAL RANG OUT WITH AMBULANCE SIRENS. A TERRIBLE RHYTHM RULED LIFE IN THE SQUARE:
WITH CLOCKWORK REGULARITY, A HUNGER STRIKER ON THE VERGE OF LOSING CONSCIOUSNESS WAS EVACUATED.

STEP ASIDE! COMING THROUGH!

AT THE HOSPITAL, THEY WERE GIVEN GLUCOSE TO STABILIZE THEIR CONDITION. THEN THE STRETCHER BEARERS WOULD BRING THEM BACK TO TIANANMEN AND CART SOMEONE ELSE OFF. AND SO THE SIRENS' HOWL TORE THROUGH THE CITY AND THE HEARTS OF ITS INHABITANTS.

THESE SIRENS KEPT PEOPLE AWARE OF THE STUDENTS' SACRIFICE. EVERYONE PITCHED IN TO SHOW THEIR SUPPORT. TAXIS WAIVED THEIR FARES, RESIDENTS SHARED WHAT LITTLE THEY HAD: BLANKETS, WATER...

THERE'S BEEN A LOT OF THEORIZING ABOUT THIS ASPECT OF THE STORY: THAT THE HUNGER STRIKE TOOK ON A UNIQUE DIMENSION IN A COUNTRY THAT HAD SUFFERED SO MANY FAMINES, WHERE RICE HAD A SYMBOLIC, ALMOST MYSTICAL ASPECT. IF YOU ASK ME, THESE PEOPLE WERE SIMPLY KIND AND GENEROUS. EVERYONE WAS MOVED BY THE HUNGER STRIKERS.

FROM THE DESTITUTE... TO THE PRIVILEGED.

THE MAELSTROM OF THE CHINESE CENTURY HAD RESULTED IN SOME SURPRISING FATES. DURING THE CULTURAL REVOLUTION, *WAN RUNNAN* WAS FORCED TO QUIT ENGINEERING SCHOOL TO LAY RAILROAD TRACKS. UNDER DENG XIAOPING, HE WAS ABLE TO GET BACK ON HIS FEET, BUILD THE STONE CORPORATION, AND BECOME CHINA'S INFORMATION TECHNOLOGY PIONEER, AMASSING A SMALL FORTUNE ALONG THE WAY.

AS AN ENTREPRENEUR, I BENEFITED FROM THE ECONOMIC REFORMS. LIKE YOU, I'VE NOTICED THAT THEY CAME TO A VIRTUAL HALT TWO YEARS AGO. HOW MAY I BE OF ASSISTANCE?

WE NEED MONEY, NATURALLY. BUT MORE URGENTLY, WE NEED EQUIPMENT.

WE'RE SHORT ON FOOD, WATER, BLANKETS...

VERY WELL. YOU CAN COUNT ON ME.

YOU ARE WARM-HEARTED, CHAI LING. TRY TO KEEP A COOL HEAD.

IN THE WEEKS THAT FOLLOWED, WAN RUNNAN AIDED THE STUDENTS SIGNIFICANTLY. HE SUPPLIED FOOD AS WELL AS STERILIZATION EQUIPMENT, RADIOS, FAX MACHINES... A SPECIAL GROUP WAS EVEN FORMED TO DEAL WITH HIM. THE STONE CORPORATION BECAME TIANANMEN SQUARE'S "HIDDEN BACKER."

THE DAYS WENT BY. THE MOVEMENT TOOK ON SCOPE. CHENGDU, SHANGHAI, KUNMING, CHONGQING... VIRTUALLY ALL OF CHINA'S MAJOR CITIES HAD THEIR OWN TIANANMENS. YOUNG PEOPLE EVERYWHERE WERE TAKING TO THE STREETS TO DEMAND GREATER DEMOCRACY AND LESS CORRUPTION. EVERY DAY, I SAW NEW STUDENTS FROM OUT IN THE COUNTRYSIDE SHOWING UP AT THE SQUARE. FOR SOME, IT WAS THEIR FIRST TIME AWAY FROM THEIR HOMETOWNS.

AS ABRAHAM LINCOLN SAID, "YOU CAN FOOL ALL THE PEOPLE SOME OF THE TIME AND SOME OF THE PEOPLE ALL THE TIME..."

"...BUT YOU CAN'T FOOL ALL THE PEOPLE ALL THE TIME!"

YOUR ENGLISH IS REALLY GOOD! WHERE ARE YOU FROM?

XI'AN. MY MAJOR IS ENGLISH LITERATURE.

ACTUALLY... THIS IS MY FIRST TIME IN BEIJING.

WELCOME TO THE BEIJING COMMUNE, COMRADE!

SANITATION WAS NOW AN ISSUE IN TIANANMEN: WASTE TO CLEAR OUT, A LACK OF TOILETS...

SOON AN ESSENTIAL QUESTION CAME UP: HOW LONG WERE WE GOING TO STAY?

I UNDERSTAND YOUR DETERMINATION TO MOVE CHINA FORWARD. I ADMIRE IT, EVEN. BUT POLITICS TAKES TIME. AND THIS HUNGER STRIKE HAS RAISED THE STAKES.

I MYSELF AM HUNGER STRIKING OUT OF SOLIDARITY WITH THE STUDENTS.

BUT I ASK YOU THIS: HOW DO YOU SEE THIS ENDING?

AMONG POLITICIANS, THE REFORMERS FELT THE DANGER OF A NEVERENDING HUNGER STRIKE RISING. THEY SUMMONED INTELLECTUALS ZHU DUO, WANG JUNTAO, WANG CHACHUA, AND LIU XIAOBO, ASKING THEM TO INTERVENE WITH THE STUDENTS, REPRESENTED BY CHAI LING.

IT'S NOT OUR JOB TO END THIS!

ALL WE'RE ASKING FOR IS OPEN DIALOGUE, AND OUR MOVEMENT TO BE RECOGNIZED AS LEGITIMATE.

NOTHING'S CHANGED! ABSOLUTELY NOTHING!

LOOK, YOU'VE MADE HISTORY! I'M BEGGING YOU— PLEASE DON'T TURN BACK THE CLOCK!

WHAT DO YOU THINK, XIAOBO?

YES, HISTORY IS MOVING FORWARD... BUT I STAND BY THE STUDENTS, NO MATTER THEIR DECISION.

LIU XIAOBO, FUTURE NOBEL PEACE PRIZE WINNER, HAD JUST RETURNED TO BEIJING AFTER SOME TIME IN THE U.S.

63

DAY 33. THURSDAY, MAY 18.

PRIME MINISTER LI PENG FINALLY AGREED TO MEET WITH A DELEGATION. THEIR DIALOGUE WAS BROADCAST ON TV.

HEIR APPARENT OF THE REGIME, LI PENG HAD MADE HIS ENTIRE CAREER IN THE WAKE OF HISTORICAL REVOLUTIONARIES. A SOVIET-STYLE TECHNOCRAT, THE ADOPTED SON AND PROTÉGÉ OF ZHOU ENLAI, HE WAS AMONG THE FEW LEADERS TO HAVE ESCAPED THE CULTURAL REVOLUTION UNSCATHED.

HE WAS IMMEDIATELY NAMED HEAD OF THE STATE EDUCATION COMMISSION, WHERE HIS FIRST ACT WAS TO REINTRODUCE IDEOLOGICAL CRITERIA TO THE UNIVERSITY ADMISSIONS PROCESS. IN OTHER WORDS, NOT A MAN WITH A SENSE OF HUMOR.

BUT WITH A SHOCKING BLEND OF DISREGARD AND INSOLENCE, WU'ER KAIXI DECIDED TO GO TO THE MEETING... WEARING A HOSPITAL GOWN!

PLEASE FORGIVE ME FOR BEING FIVE MINUTES LATE. YOU'VE NO DOUBT NOTICED BEIJING TRAFFIC IS A BIT BACKED UP THESE DAYS.

THINK NOTHING OF IT. YOU'RE NOT FIVE MINUTES LATE...

...YOU'RE A WHOLE MONTH LATE!

ZHAO ZIYANG'S FALL FROM GRACE A FEW HOURS EARLIER HAD DOOMED THE ENTIRE MOVEMENT.

BUT IN THE SQUARE, NO ONE NOTICES THAT DENG XIAOPING HAS JUST TURNED THE HOURGLASS.

THE PATRIARCH HAD GATHERED HIS GENERALS AROUND HIM. WAS MARTIAL LAW NECESSARY? BESIDE LI PENG WAS PRESIDENT OF THE REPUBLIC, YANG SHANGKUN. ACROSS FROM THEM SAT REFORMER ZHAO ZIYANG. DEFEATED, HE PLAYED HIS LAST CARD.

THE MOST IMPORTANT THING RIGHT NOW IS TO GET THE STUDENTS OUT OF THE SQUARE AND BACK TO THEIR CAMPUSES.

COMRADE ZIYANG IS IN LARGE PART RESPONSIBLE FOR THIS SITUATION. HE SHOWED LENIENCE AND PUBLICLY CONTRADICTED THE PARTY'S POSITIONS.

WE MUST PUT AN END TO THIS MOVEMENT AS SOON AS WE CAN!

AFTER THINKING LONG AND HARD ABOUT THIS, I'VE CONCLUDED THAT WE SHOULD BRING IN THE PEOPLE'S LIBERATION ARMY AND DECLARE MARTIAL LAW IN BEIJING.

IT'S ALWAYS BETTER TO HAVE A DECISION THAN NOT TO HAVE ONE. BUT IT WILL BE HARD FOR ME TO CARRY OUT THIS PLAN. I HAVE DIFFICULTIES WITH IT.

THE MINORITY YIELDS TO THE MAJORITY!

I WILL SUBMIT TO PARTY DISCIPLINE. THE MINORITY DOES YIELD TO THE MAJORITY.

ZHAO WAS AWARE HE'D LOST THE ROUND, AND HE KNEW THE RULES: HIS POLITICAL CAREER WAS OVER.

WITH HIM, THE LAST LINK BETWEEN DENG AND THE STUDENTS HAD BEEN SEVERED.

AT 4 A.M. ON MAY 19, WE SAW ZHAO ZIYANG FOR THE LAST TIME, AT THE SQUARE. HIS VOICE FALTERED, HIS EYES MISTED OVER. WE DIDN'T KNOW IT THEN, BUT HE'D COME TO TELL US GOODBYE.

ZHAO ZIYANG ENDED HIS DAYS UNDER HOUSE ARREST A STONE'S THROW FROM TIANANMEN.

WE HAVE COME TOO LATE. WE DEMONSTRATED AND LAY ACROSS RAILROAD TRACKS WHEN WE WERE YOUNG, TOO, WITHOUT A THOUGHT FOR THE FUTURE.

NOW WE ARE OLD. OUR FATE NO LONGER MATTERS. BUT YOU—YOU ARE YOUNG! I MUST ASK YOU TO THINK CAREFULLY ABOUT YOUR HEALTH, YOUR FUTURE! BEG YOU TO END THIS HUNGER STRIKE!

I'VE HAD A LOT OF TIME TO PONDER THOSE FEW WEEKS IN MAY. NOW I KNOW IT'S TRUE WHAT THEY SAY: THE WINNERS WRITE THE HISTORY.

IN 1989, WE THOUGHT WE WERE MAKING HISTORY, MOVING TOWARD THE FUTURE. BUT IN REALITY, THE PARTY WAS ALWAYS BUSY REWRITING, WINDING BACK THE CLOCK.

XINHUA, THE STATE NEWS AGENCY, SPARED ONLY THESE TWO SENTENCES ABOUT ZHAO WHEN HE DIED IN 2005: "DURING THE PERIODS OF CHINA'S OPENING AND REFORM, COMRADE ZHAO ZIYANG SERVED THE PARTY AND THE STATE IN AN IMPORTANT CAPACITY, AND CONTRIBUTED IN A VALUABLE WAY TO THE PARTY AND THE PEOPLE. BUT DURING THE PERIOD OF POLITICAL TURMOIL IN THE SPRING AND SUMMER OF 1989, COMRADE ZHAO MADE SOME SERIOUS MISTAKES."

ACT IV
-MARTIAL LAW-

ORDER OF THE BEIJING MUNICIPAL PEOPLE'S GOVERNMENT:
NUMBER 3, MAY 20

1) BEGINNING AT 10 A.M. ON MAY 20, 1989, THE FOLLOWING
DISTRICTS WILL BE UNDER MARTIAL LAW: EAST CITY, WEST
CITY, CHONGWEN, XUANWU, SHIJINGSHAN, HAIDIAN, FENGTAI,
AND CHAOYANG.

2) UNDER MARTIAL LAW, DEMONSTRATIONS, STUDENT
STRIKES, WORK STOPPAGES, AND ALL OTHER ACTIVITIES
THAT IMPEDE PUBLIC ORDER ARE BANNED.

3) PEOPLE ARE FORBIDDEN FROM FABRICATING OR
SPREADING RUMORS, NETWORKING, MAKING PUBLIC
SPEECHES, DISTRIBUTING LEAFLETS, OR INCITING
SOCIAL TURMOIL.

4) ASSAULT ON LEADERSHIP ORGANS OF THE PARTY,
GOVERNMENT, OR ARMY, ON RADIO OR TELEVISION STATIONS,
OR ON COMMUNICATIONS UNITS AND SABOTAGE OF KEY
PUBLIC FACILITIES IS EXPRESSLY FORBIDDEN. NO FORMS
OF DESTRUCTION WILL BE TOLERATED.

5) HARASSING FOREIGN EMBASSIES OR AGENCIES
OF THE UNITED NATIONS IS PROHIBITED.

6) UNDER MARTIAL LAW, SECURITY OFFICERS, PAP, AND PLA
SOLDIERS ARE AUTHORIZED TO USE ALL NECESSARY MEANS,
INCLUDING FORCE, TO DEAL WITH PROHIBITED ACTIVITIES.

STARTING TONIGHT, MARTIAL LAW HAS BEEN DECLARED IN CERTAIN DISTRICTS OF BEIJING.

ALL GATHERINGS OF ANY KIND ARE NOW STRICTLY FORBIDDEN!

WHAT DOES THIS MEAN?

IT MEANS THE ARMY'LL TURN UP ANY MINUTE NOW.

SUDDENLY, I HEARD A TREMENDOUS ROARING OF ENGINES. THIS WAS IT: IT WAS ALL OVER. THE ARMY'S TRUCKS WERE HEADED FOR TIANANMEN...

THEN I SAW THE BEAMS OF HEADLIGHTS PIERCING THE DARK...

VROOOOOOOOM

VROOOOOM

ARE YOU IN CHARGE HERE?

WE'RE FROM THE BEIJING MOTORCYCLE BRIGADE, AND WE'VE GOT SOME GOOD NEWS!

THE ARMY TRIED TO ENTER THE CITY, BUT THEY'VE BEEN BLOCKED ALL OVER! THE PEOPLE OF BEIJING ARE PROTECTING YOU AND KEEPING THEM FROM ADVANCING!

I THANKED THESE MESSENGERS, BEGGING THEM NOT TO RIDE AROUND IN SUCH NUMBERS. THE NOISE THEY MADE HAD SET OFF A PANIC. THAT NIGHT, THE MOVEMENT'S PEACE OF MIND SEEMED TO HANG BY A THREAD...

69

DAY 35. SATURDAY, MAY 20.

ROUSED FROM THEIR BARRACKS, THE SOLDIERS HAD BEEN EXPECTING AGGRESSIVE DEMONSTRATORS, HORDES OF COUNTERREVOLUTIONARY HOOLIGANS. WHAT THEY FOUND INSTEAD WERE MEN AND WOMEN WHO COULD'VE BEEN THEIR FRIENDS, AUNTS, OR UNCLES. IN OTHER CIRCUMSTANCES, WITHOUT THEIR HELMETS AND UNIFORMS, THEY COULD'VE BEEN ON THE SAME SIDE.

THEY LIED TO YOU! BEIJING IS NOT IN CHAOS.

COMRADES OF THE PEOPLE'S ARMY, DO NOT FIRE ON THE PEOPLE!

SUDDENLY, THEY HAD NO MORE ENEMIES. THEY REFUSED TO FIGHT THEIR OWN FELLOWS, TO CARRY OUT THE WARLIKE ORDERS THE REGIME HAD GIVEN THEM.

JUST BEFORE THE ICONIC SHOTS OF THE TANK MAN, THESE IMAGES OF THE ARMY FRATERNIZING WITH THE PEOPLE CIRCULATED AROUND THE WORLD.

I THINK THEY TRANSCEND THE CONTEXT OF BEIJING. THEY SPEAK TO US OF WAR AND HUMANITY.

THAT IS WHY THEY MOVE US SO DEEPLY. FOR A FEW DAYS, BEIJING WAS A UTOPIA.

SINCE THE ARMY HAD COME TO A STANDSTILL, THE REGIME WAS REDUCED TO TOSSING OUT TRACTS. A HARMLESS SHOWER OF PAPER THAT ONLY FANNED THE FLAMES OF OUR RESOLVE TO STAY.

DOWN WITH LI PENG!

LI PENG, YOU BASTARD!

RESIGN, LI PENG!

99 LUFTBALLONS. AUF IHREM WEG ZUM HORIZONT ...

THANKS TO THE BRAVE PEOPLE OF BEIJING, THE ONLY UNIFORMS I SAW MARCHING INTO TIANANMEN BELONGED TO POLICEMEN ON STRIKE WHO'D JOINED OUR CAUSE!

ON MAY 21, AT THE FOOT OF THE MONUMENT TO THE PEOPLE'S HEROES, WE SYMBOLICALLY CELEBRATED THE MARRIAGE OF LI LU, A STUDENT FROM NANKIN, AND HIS GIRLFRIEND. THERE WAS NO ORGAN, BUT THE STUDENTS DELIVERED A ROUSING CHORUS OF THE "WEDDING MARCH"... AND "THE INTERNATIONALE"!

WE EVEN PUT UP A SPECIAL TENT FOR THE YOUNG NEWLYWEDS' WEDDING NIGHT. THE PANIC OVER MARTIAL LAW HAD GIVEN WAY TO JUBILATION. FROM MY OBSERVATION POST, I SAW NEW STUDENTS ARRIVE AT THE SQUARE EVERY DAY.

AND YET, AT THAT VERY MOMENT, I BEGAN TO FEEL THE MOVEMENT STARTING TO SPLINTER.

72

DAY 38. TUESDAY, MAY 23.

HOW LONG HAD IT BEEN SINCE I'D SLEPT? I SPENT MY DAYS FIGHTING MY OWN BODY, WHICH WAS SCREAMING TO LIE DOWN. SOMETIMES I MANAGED TO SNATCH A FEW SECONDS OF SHUTEYE.

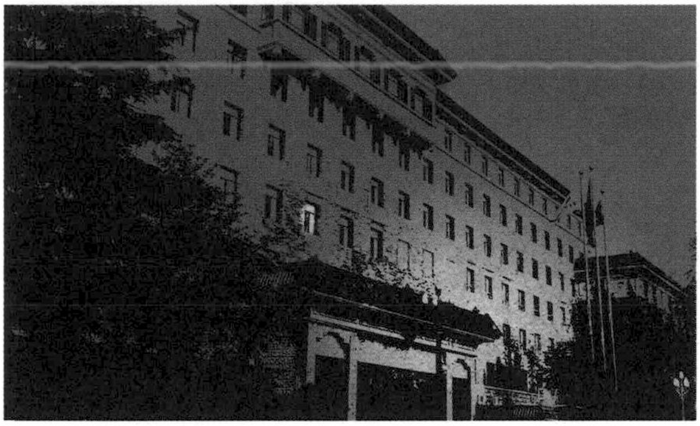

AROUND ME, THE WORLD WAS FLICKERING LIKE A STROBELIGHT. BUT I HAD TO KEEP MY EYES OPEN. THIS MEETING WAS IMPORTANT.

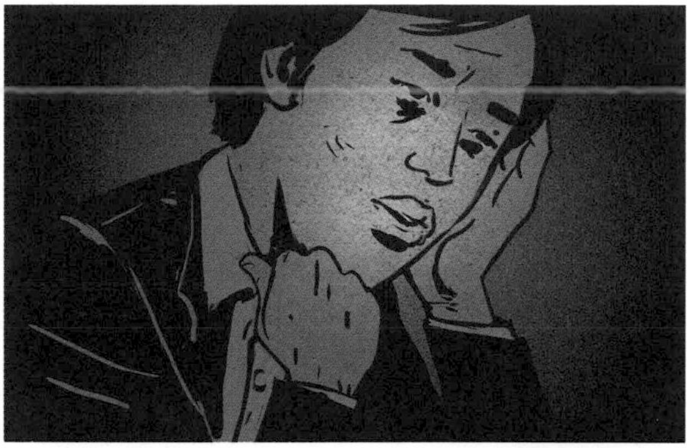

IT WAS HIGH TIME TO GIVE THE MOVEMENT SOME STRUCTURE. IN A ROOM AT THE ACADEMY OF SOCIAL SCIENCES, WANG JUNTAO AND CHEN ZIMING, TWO VETERAN ACTIVISTS OF THE DEMOCRACY WALL, HAD ASSEMBLED REPRESENTATIVES FROM VARIOUS UNIONS: STUDENTS, BEIJING RESIDENTS, WORKERS, AND INTELLECTUALS.

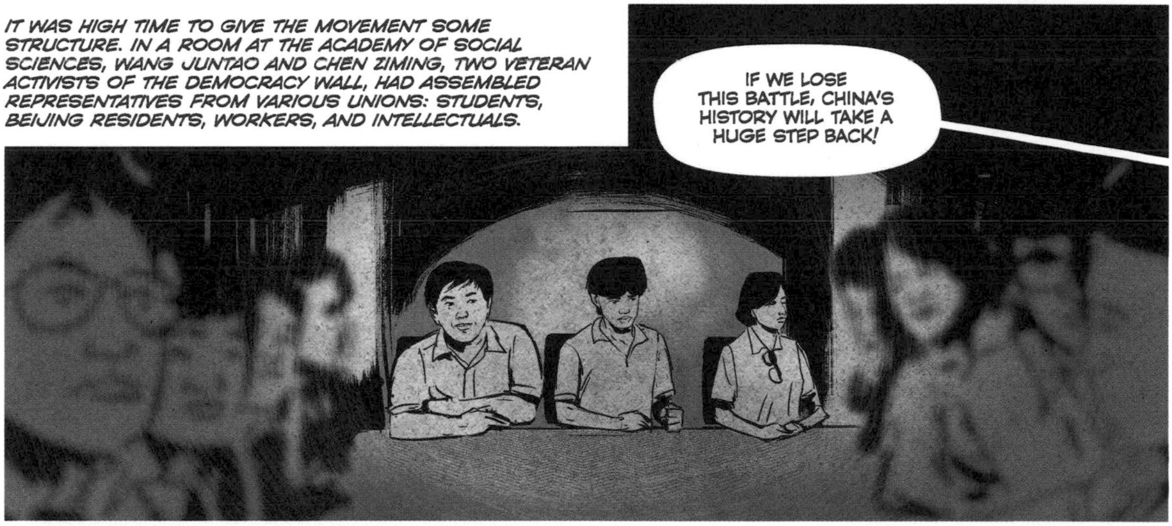
IF WE LOSE THIS BATTLE, CHINA'S HISTORY WILL TAKE A HUGE STEP BACK!

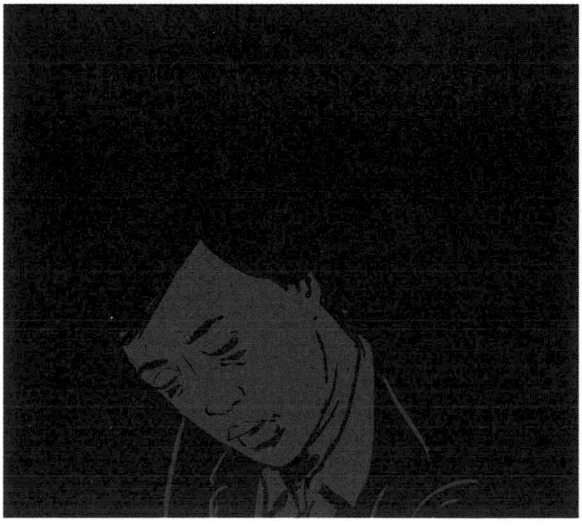

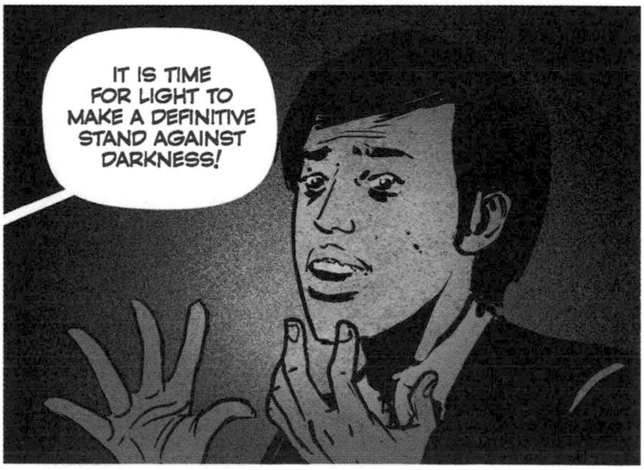
IT IS TIME FOR LIGHT TO MAKE A DEFINITIVE STAND AGAINST DARKNESS!

EVERYONE WAS WORN OUT, BUT GALVANIZED BY WHAT THEY WERE WITNESSING. THAT AFTERNOON, WE FOUNDED THE "DEFEND TIANANMEN SQUARE HEADQUARTERS."

IT INCLUDED DEPARTMENTS FOR COMMUNICATIONS, PUBLIC RELATIONS, AND WELCOMING STUDENTS FROM THE PROVINCES, ETC. BETWEEN TWO BOUTS OF NODDING OFF, I AGREED TO BE THE DIRECTOR IN CHARGE OF MAINTAINING ORDER, A POST I HELD FOR THE NEXT DOZEN DAYS.

MY TITLE WON ME A SPOT ON THE COUNTRY'S MOST WANTED LIST. THE PARTY BELIEVED I WAS SOME SORT OF GENERAL, A MENACING TACTICIAN FOR A COUNTERREVOLUTIONARY MOVEMENT.

CHAI LING WOULD OVERSEE THE ORGANIZATION, AND TOOK ON THE DAUNTING ROLE OF "COMMANDER-IN-CHIEF OF DEFEND TIANANMEN SQUARE HEADQUARTERS". WHENEVER I MANAGED TO KEEP MY EYES OPEN, I SAW HER BEAMING LIKE A PRINCESS ON CORONATION DAY.

LITTLE DID WE KNOW WE HAD JUST COMMITTED THE GRAVEST OF CRIMES IN THE PARTY'S EYES. WE HAD OFFICIALLY INSTITUTED AN OPPOSING POWER.

MAO WAS BORN IN HUNAN, AND PEOPLE FROM THAT PROVINCE HAD A REPUTATION FOR BEING HOTHEADED. DURING OUR MEETING, THREE OF THEM DEFACED THE PORTRAIT OF THE GREAT HELMSMAN.

IT WAS A PREMEDITATED ACT. THEY HAD FILLED EGGSHELLS WITH INK TO HURL AGAINST THE FORBIDDEN CITY'S FAÇADE.

WHEN I REACHED THE SQUARE, STUDENTS ANXIOUS TO KEEP THE MOVEMENT SAFE HAD TURNED THE HUNANESE OVER TO THE AUTHORITIES. ALL THREE RECEIVED LENGTHY PRISON SENTENCES.

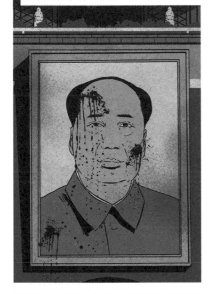

YU ZHIJIAN WAS RELEASED IN SEPTEMBER 2000 AND OBTAINED ASYLUM IN THE U.S. RECENTLY, I LEARNED HE HAD DIED.

LU DECHENG SECRETLY FLED CHINA AND FOUND REFUGE IN CANADA.

BY THE TIME YU DONGYUE WAS RELEASED IN 2006, HE'D BEEN DRIVEN MAD BY MISTREATMENT AND TORTURE.

I WATCHED THE INK TRICKLE DOWN MAO'S PORTRAIT AND SUDDENLY, I FELT DIZZY.

I DON'T KNOW IF IT WAS EXHAUSTION, OR THE WIND PICKING UP.

SOMETIMES SANDSTORMS FROM MONGOLIA WOULD SWEEP OVER BEIJING.

DOWN WITH LI PENG

DOWN WITH DICT

THE NEXT DAY, THE STORM HAD SUBSIDED, BUT I WAS STILL DIZZY. WE HAD PLANNED TO SWEAR AN OATH IN TIANANMEN SQUARE, AND I LISTENED TO CHAI LING, CAUGHT UP IN HER LYRICISM.

...TO PROTECT THE DIGNITY OF THE CONSTITUTION, TO PROTECT THE GREAT MOTHERLAND FROM THE MACHINATIONS OF A SMALL HANDFUL OF CONSPIRATORS...

...TO PREVENT 1.1 BILLION COUNTRYMEN FROM BEING SACRIFICED IN BLOOD UNDER THE TERROR OF MILITARY RULE, TO SAVE THE CHINESE PEOPLE FROM FALLING UNDER FASCIST DICTATORIAL RULE, TO...

I SWEAR TO DEVOTE MY LIFE AND MY LOYALTY TO PROTECT TO THE DEATH TIANANMEN SQUARE, THE CAPITAL BEIJING, AND THE REPUBLIC. STRUGGLE TO THE END AGAINST ALL DIFFICULTIES!

LONG LIVE DEMOCRACY!

LI PENG, YOU PUPPET! RESIGN!

HURRAH!!

NOW SLUNG ACROSS MY CHEST WAS A HANDSOME SASH EMBLAZONED WITH MY TITLE. I SPENT HOURS SIGNING SAFE CONDUCTS AND AUTHORIZATIONS THAT ALLOWED THEIR BEARERS TO MOVE FREELY ABOUT THE SQUARE. WE WANTED ABOVE ALL TO SHOW THAT WE WERE IN CONTROL OF THE SITUATION.

THE LANDSCAPE ALL AROUND ME HAD CHANGED. STUDENTS FROM HONG KONG HAD SHOWN UP WITH HIGH-TECH TENTS THAT COULD BE PITCHED IN THE BLINK OF AN EYE. THEY GAVE ME A FABULOUS PAIR OF INFRARED BINOCULARS. I COULD SEE CLEARLY IN THE DARK. BUT NEVER HAD THE FUTURE SEEMED SO HAZY. I HAD NO IDEA WHERE ANY OF THIS WOULD LEAD US. MY KNEES WERE ALWAYS ABOUT TO BUCKLE.

ROCK STAR CUI JIAN WAS THERE TOO. RECENT EVENTS HAD GIVEN HIS SONG "NOTHING TO MY NAME" NEW MEANING.

YOU LAUGH WHEN I SAY I HAVE NOTHING, NOTHING BUT MY NAME!

CONVENTIONAL WISDOM SUGGESTED WE LEAVE THE SQUARE BEFORE IT WAS TOO LATE. MY HONG KONG BINOCULARS TOLD ME SOMETHING ELSE: A GOOD NUMBER OF STUDENTS WANTED TO STAY.

WHEN WILL YOU COME WITH ME?

WHEN WILL YOU COME WITH ME?

YES, WE HAVE NOTHING BUT OUR NAMES! WHEN WILL WE GO?

THE DEBATE AMONG THE LEADERS WAS GROWING HEATED. MORE OR LESS UNITED UP TILL NOW, THE INTELLECTUALS REPRESENTED BY WANG JUNTAO AND THE MOST VEHEMENT STUDENTS LED BY CHAI LING WEREN'T GETTING ALONG ANYMORE.

THIS ISN'T FRANCE FROM TWO CENTURIES AGO! THE STREET CANNOT TRIUMPH OVER THE AUTHORITIES! WE MUST LEAVE THE SQUARE TO KEEP WHAT WE'VE WON!

WHAT WE'VE WON? WHAT IS THAT, EXACTLY? NONE OF OUR DEMANDS WERE GRANTED!

EVERY DAY BRINGS US CLOSER TO A CONFRONTATION! THE PEOPLE SUPPORT US. WE MUST FIND OTHER WAYS TO KEEP UP THE FIGHT!

ALL YOU INTELLECTUALS EVER DO IS TALK! LEAVING IS GIVING UP! DON'T YOU GET IT?

NO, CHAI LING! YOU'RE THE ONE WHO DOESN'T GET IT!

WE'VE ALREADY WON!

ON MAY 27, WE DECIDED TO EVACUATE THE SQUARE WITHIN THREE DAYS...

...AFTER ONE FINAL DISPLAY OF FORCE.

THAT DECISION HAD NO REAL EFFECT.

WHEN A LARGE COLLECTIVE ACTION HAS NO STRUCTURE, THE MOST RADICAL VOICES ALWAYS WIN OUT OVER THE MODERATES.

I VAGUELY REMEMBER COLLAPSING. I WOKE TO A PALE GLOW AND THE REEK OF ETHER.
I MUST'VE BEEN TAKEN TO THE HOSPITAL WHEN MY LEGS GAVE OUT.

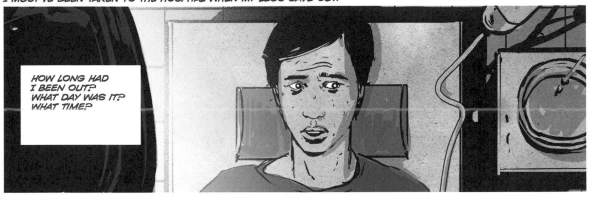

HOW LONG HAD
I BEEN OUT?
WHAT DAY WAS IT?
WHAT TIME?

I WAS AT QIANMEN HOSPITAL, SOUTH OF THE SQUARE. NO ONE ASKED ME ANY QUESTIONS, SO I STARTED WALKING
HOME, THE STRANGEST WALK OF MY LIFE. FOR THE FIRST TIME IN WEEKS, I'D LEFT THE HOTHOUSE OF THE SQUARE.
I WAS BACK IN THE FAMILIAR STREETS OF BEIJING, THE WARM AIR OF A CITY READYING FOR SUMMER. NOTHING HAD
CHANGED. LIFE WENT ON AS USUAL.

I CROSSED A SILENT CAMPUS. LAST YEAR AT THIS TIME, EVERYONE HAD BEEN STUDYING FOR EXAMS.

SUDDENLY, I REALIZED
SOMETHING BLINDINGLY
OBVIOUS: MY FRIENDS
AND I WERE ABOUT TO
GO UNDERGROUND, INTO
HIDING, AND INEVITABLY,
IN A FEW DAYS MANY
OF US WOULD BE IN
JAIL. I DECIDED TO
WRITE MY ROOMMATE
A BRIEF NOTE.

MY FRIEND,

IF I GET ARRESTED
TOMORROW MORNING,
I BEG YOU TO FIND A
WAY TO TELL MY MOTHER
THAT WON'T UPSET HER.
PLEASE BE CAREFUL, AS
SHE HAS A WEAK HEART.

AS FOR ME, YOU KNOW
THE PRESCRIPTION I'VE
BEEN TAKING FOR A YEAR
NOW TO TREAT MY ULCER.
I TRUST YOU'LL FIND A
WAY TO GET THEM TO
ME IN PRISON.

THROUGH THE WINDOW,
I WATCHED THE LAST
LIGHT OF DAY SETTLE
ON THE UNIVERSITY'S
QUADS AND SQUARES.

THE TREES WERE
IN FLOWER, THE
BIRDS SOARING
PAST IN AN
ORANGE SKY...

AND I THOUGHT
THEN THAT THIS
MIGHT BE THE
LAST TIME I
BEHELD SUCH A
BEAUTIFUL SUNSET.

XU, WHAT'S YOUR FAVORITE SONG ABOUT?

IT'S ABOUT 99 VERY BEAUTIFUL BALLOONS FLOATING UP TOWARD THE HORIZON...

SOME DUMB GENERAL MISTAKES THE BALLOONS FOR A UFO INVASION AND SENDS OUT JETS TO STOP IT.

WHEN ANOTHER STUPID GENERAL SEES THOSE PLANES, HE SENDS OUT HIS OWN SQUADRON.

AN ABSURD AND MURDEROUS WAR ENSUES.

BUT ALL THERE EVER WERE IN THE SKY WERE 99 BALLOONS...

DAY 45. TUESDAY, MAY 30.

PUT TOGETHER IN FOUR DAYS BY STUDENTS FROM THE CENTRAL ACADEMY OF FINE ARTS, THE "GODDESS OF DEMOCRACY" PROVED THE FINAL INITIATIVE IN THE LONG WAR OF SYMBOLS THAT MARKED THE PASSING OF THAT SPRING. THOUGH THE SQUARE HAD BEGUN TO EMPTY, THE STATUE, THE LATEST AUDACIOUS MONUMENT RAISED AGAINST MAO, DREW A NEW ROUND OF ONLOOKERS, PARENTS AND CHILDREN, LIKE A TOURIST TRAP.

THE NEXT DAY, THE PEOPLE'S DAILY RESPONDED WITH A FURIOUS EDITORIAL. IN HINDSIGHT, IT READ LIKE A WARNING: "ALL CITIZENS MUST CHERISH AND PROTECT TIANANMEN SQUARE, JUST AS THEY CHERISH AND DEFEND THE MOTHERLAND. THE SQUARE IS A SACRED PLACE. NO ONE HAS THE RIGHT TO ADD A MONUMENT OR DEFACE AN EXISTING ONE. SUCH THINGS CANNOT BE ALLOWED TO HAPPEN IN CHINA."

MEANWHILE, THE CAMPAIGN OF ARRESTS HAD DISCREETLY BEGUN.

IS THAT THE AMERICAN STATUE?

NO, YOU DINGDONG! CAN'T YOU SEE SHE'S CHINESE? SHE'S OUR GODDESS OF DEMOCRACY!

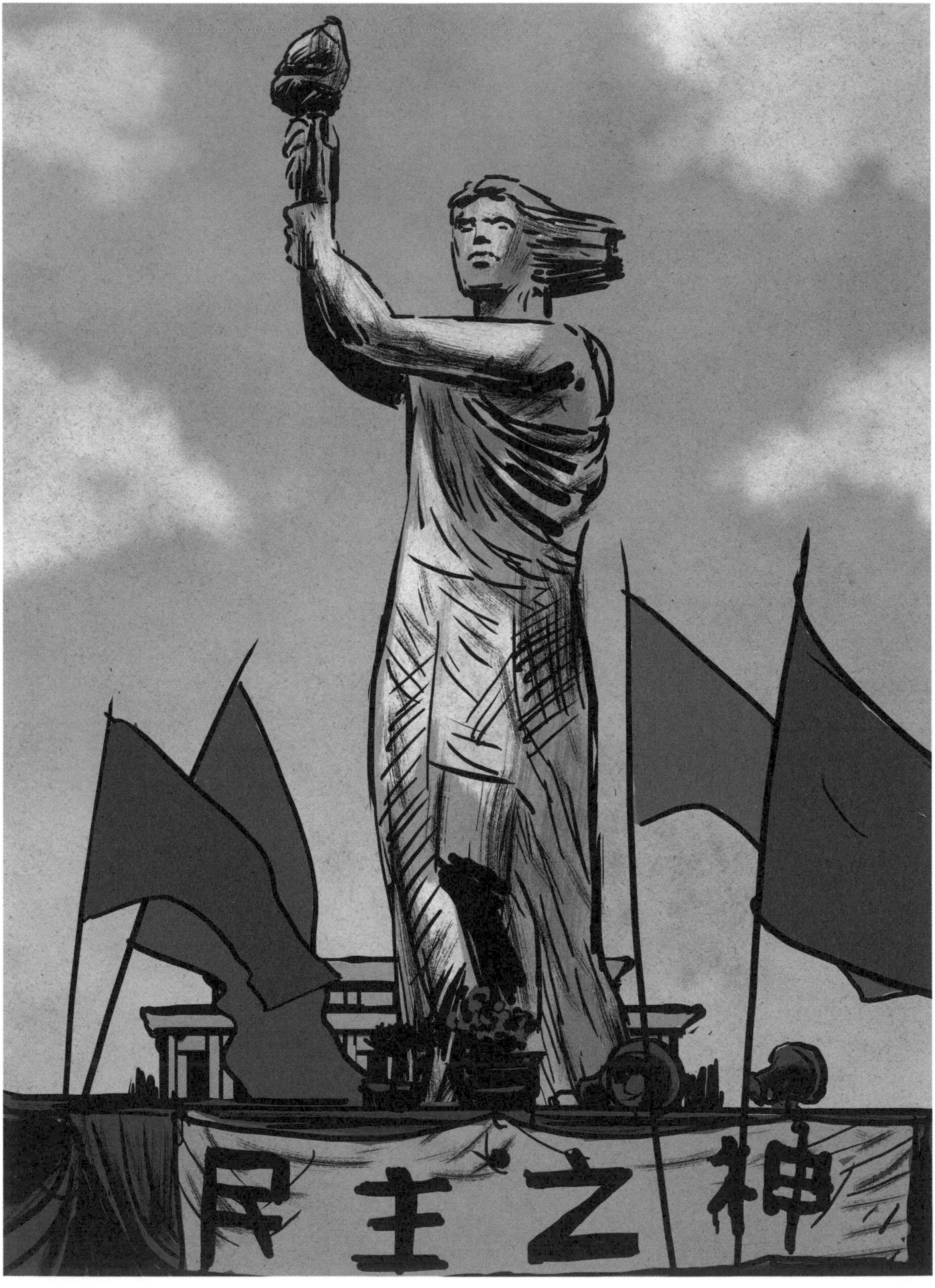
民主之神

ON JUNE 2, FOUR INTELLECTUALS—ZHOU DUO, HOU DEJIAN, GAO XIN, AND LIU XIAOBO—BEGAN A HUNGER STRIKE.

THEY HOPED TO MAKE THE STUDENTS LISTEN TO REASON AND FIND A WAY TO HALT THE ESCALATION THAT WOULD LEAD TO REPRESSION.

TO THIS END, LIU XIAOBO WOULD DELIVER THE MOST POWERFUL SPEECH OF 1989.

VERY STRONG WORDS, SIMPLE SENTENCES, THAT WOULD RESONATE FAR BEYOND THE CELL WHERE HE ENDED HIS DAYS.

WE HAVE NO ENEMIES! DO NOT LET HATRED AND VIOLENCE POISON OUR WISDOM AND THE DEMOCRATIZATION OF CHINA.

WE MUST ALL PROCEED TO EXAMINE OUR CONSCIENCE...

WE EACH BEAR OUR SHARE OF THE BLAME IN CHINA'S BACKWARDNESS.

WE ARE ALL CITIZENS. WHAT WE SEEK IS NOT DEATH BUT A LIFE TRULY LIVED.

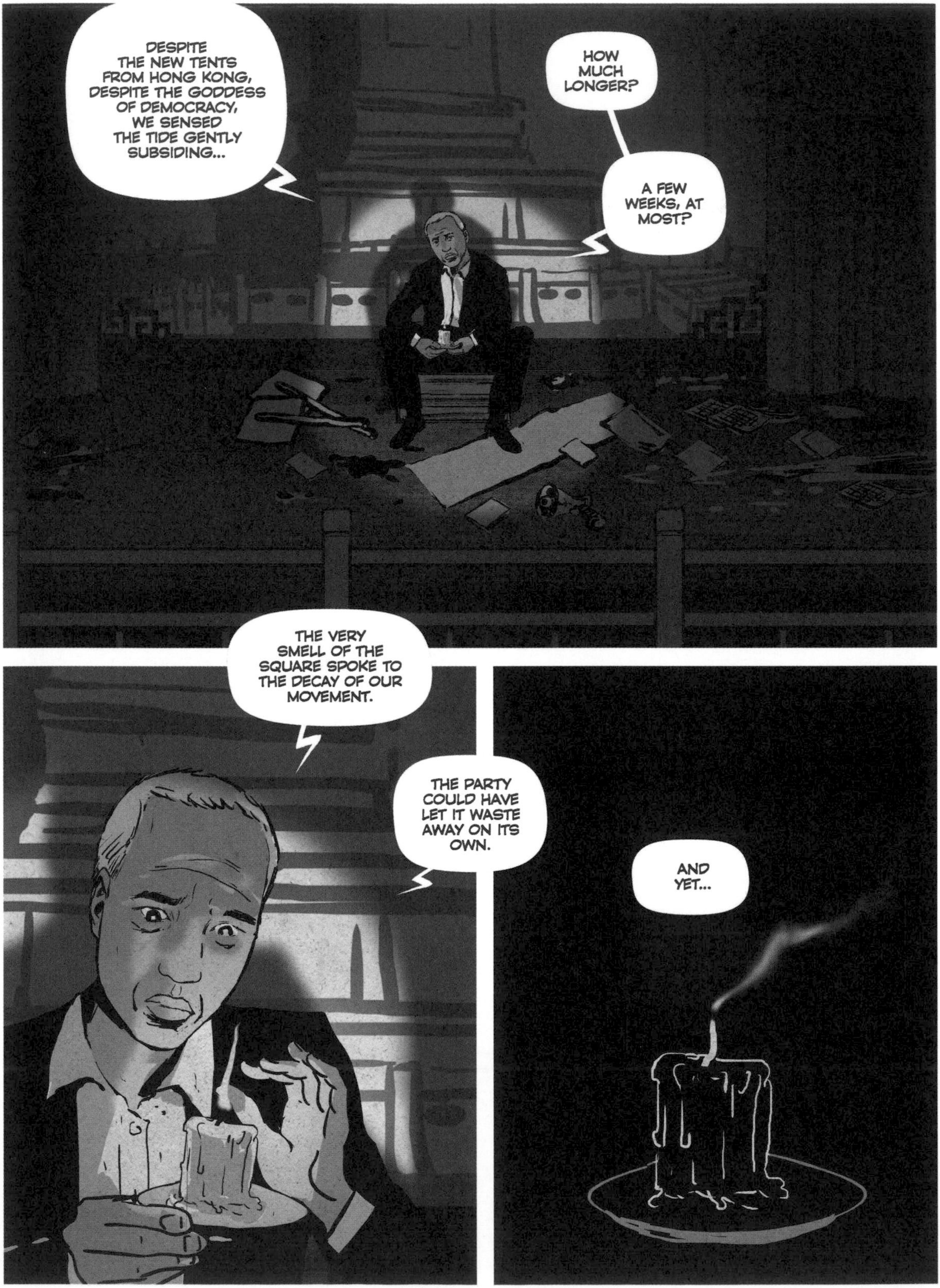

DESPITE THE NEW TENTS FROM HONG KONG, DESPITE THE GODDESS OF DEMOCRACY, WE SENSED THE TIDE GENTLY SUBSIDING...
HOW MUCH LONGER?
A FEW WEEKS, AT MOST?
THE VERY SMELL OF THE SQUARE SPOKE TO THE DECAY OF OUR MOVEMENT.
THE PARTY COULD HAVE LET IT WASTE AWAY ON ITS OWN.
AND YET...

ACT V
-THE REPRESSION-

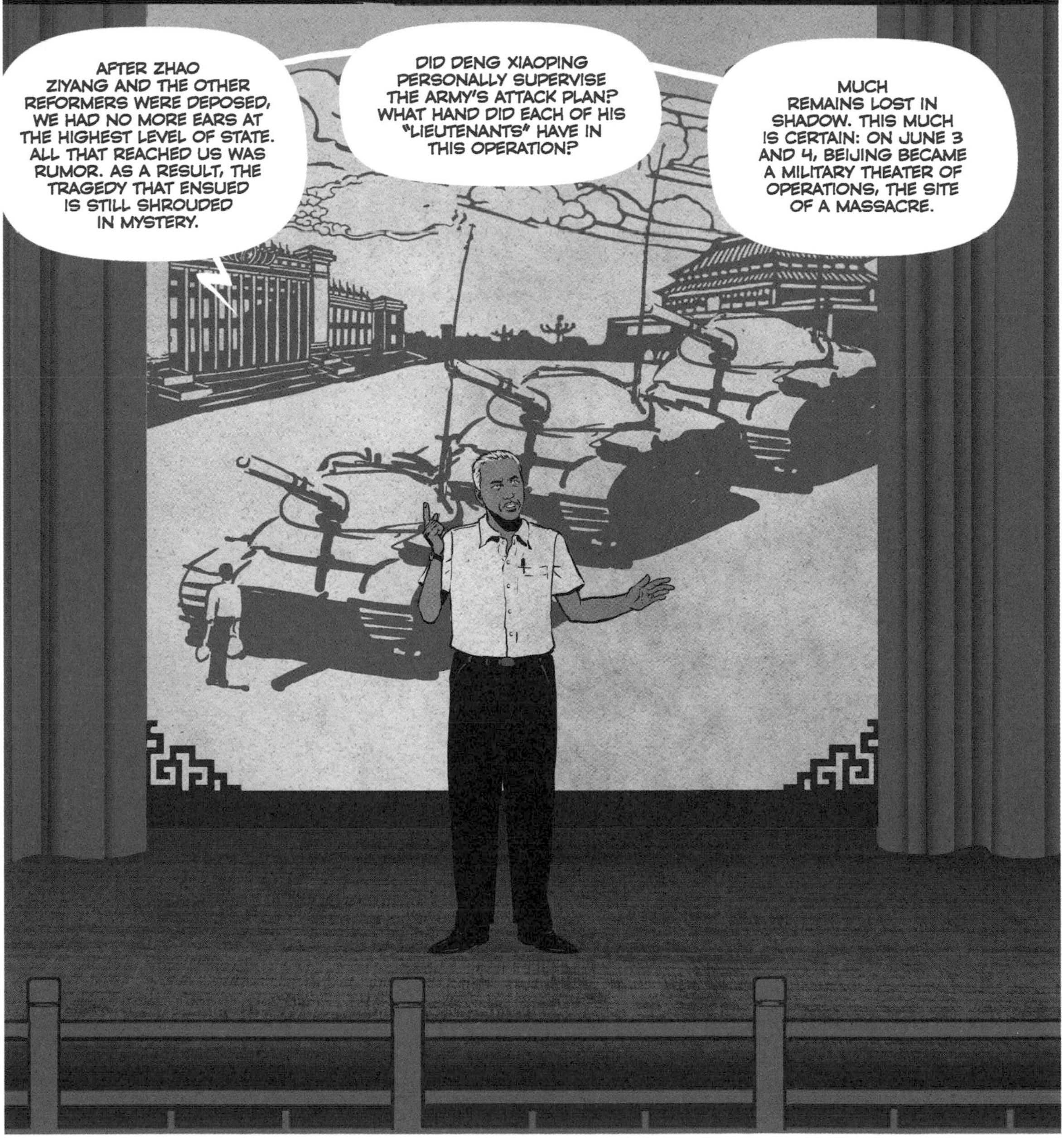

LOOK, SOMETHING'S GOING ON.

THE CROWD IS SUPER TENSE. SEEMS THEY JUST FOUND A BUS FULL OF WEAPONS.

THERE ARE SOLDIERS AND PLAINCLOTHES COPS OUT ALL OVER.

I'M GIVING YOU TWO MINUTES FOR THE EVENING NEWS. GET READY FOR SOME HEAVY STUFF LATER TODAY.

"STEPHANIE, YOU'RE ON IN 5, 4, 3, 2, 1..."

"TIANANMEN SQUARE WAS MEANT TO HOST THE INAUGURATION OF A 'UNIVERSITY OF DEMOCRACY' TONIGHT, FOLLOWED BY A CONCERT FROM HUNGER STRIKER AND SINGER HOU DEJIAN. BUT AT 4 A.M., THE LIGHTS WERE ABRUPTLY TURNED OUT.

"BUT THE BATTLE OF BEIJING HAD ACTUALLY BEGUN HOURS AGO, AND IN MUXIDI, LESS THAN SIX MILES WEST OF TIANAMEN, GUNFIRE RANG OUT.

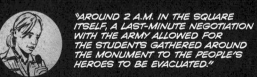

"AROUND 2 A.M. IN THE SQUARE ITSELF, A LAST-MINUTE NEGOTIATION WITH THE ARMY ALLOWED FOR THE STUDENTS GATHERED AROUND THE MONUMENT TO THE PEOPLE'S HEROES TO BE EVACUATED."

STAND UP, YE VICTIMS OF OPPRESSION...

FOR THE TYRANTS FEAR YOUR MIGHT...

THEN ALL HELL BROKE LOOSE.

 "RIGHT NOW, AS I SPEAK, TANKS HAVE SEIZED THE SQUARE AND BURSTS OF HEAVY MACHINE GUN FIRE TEAR THROUGH THE BEIJING NIGHT.

 "THERE'S NO TELLING THE NUMBER OF CASUALTIES, SHOT DOWN OR ELSE RUN OVER BY THE TANKS..."

HOLD ON, LILI, HOLD ON! WE'LL FIND YOU A DOCTOR!

"...OF WHAT NO ONE NOW DARES CALL THE PEOPLE'S LIBERATION ARMY."

IS IT OVER YET? IS THAT IT?
I DON'T KNOW. IT'S QUIET ALL OF A SUDDEN...
CUI JIAN
TACTACTAC
POW

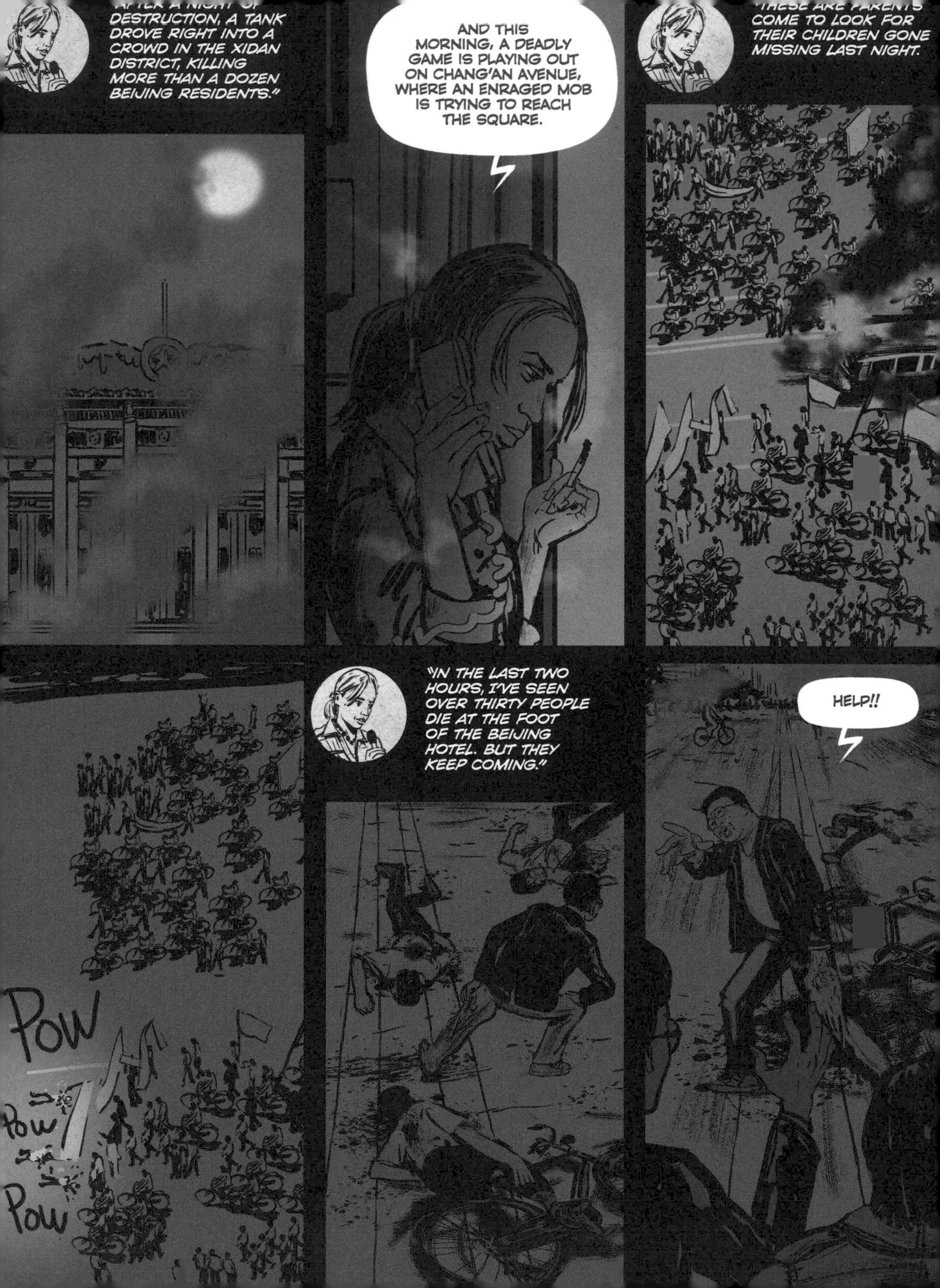
DESTRUCTION, A TANK DROVE RIGHT INTO A CROWD IN THE XIDAN DISTRICT, KILLING MORE THAN A DOZEN BEIJING RESIDENTS.”
AND THIS MORNING, A DEADLY GAME IS PLAYING OUT ON CHANG'AN AVENUE, WHERE AN ENRAGED MOB IS TRYING TO REACH THE SQUARE.
COME TO LOOK FOR THEIR CHILDREN GONE MISSING LAST NIGHT.
“IN THE LAST TWO HOURS, I'VE SEEN OVER THIRTY PEOPLE DIE AT THE FOOT OF THE BEIJING HOTEL. BUT THEY KEEP COMING.”
HELP!!
POW
POW
POW

"CHARRED BODIES, POOLS OF CLOTTED BLOOD. SPENT CASINGS. CHANG'AN AVENUE, WHOSE NAME MEANS 'LASTING PEACE,' HAS TURNED INTO A MASS GRAVE TONIGHT.

"VICTIMS NUMBER IN THE HUNDREDS, MAYBE EVEN THE THOUSANDS! THE ARMY IS ALREADY BUSY BURNING BODIES AND TRYING TO GET RID OF THE SINISTER EVIDENCE. NO MATTER THE EXACT NUMBER, BEIJING WILL FOREVER BEAR THE WOUNDS OF THIS JUNE 4TH.

"AND SO *THE BEIJING SPRING* COMES TO AN END. IN A COUNTRY THAT MAKES UP A QUARTER OF THE WORLD'S POPULATION, THE OLD REGIME IS SLAUGHTERING ITS YOUNG, BEFORE THE EYES OF THE WORLD.

"STEPHANIE ANDREWS. BBC NEWS. BEIJING."

LET US NEVER FORGET THIS DARK DAY...

JUST GOT BACK FROM THE HOSPITAL. IT'S A SLAUGHTERHOUSE BACK THERE. PURE CARNAGE. I'VE BEEN AT THIS FOR TWENTY YEARS. NEVER SEEN THIS.

THEY KILLED 'EM! THOSE BASTARDS!

THEY KILLED ALL THOSE KIDS, RIGHT IN FRONT OF US!

AND YOU KNOW WHAT? WE'RE GONNA GO HOME LIKE A BUNCH OF ASSHOLES. AND MY PHOTOS, YOUR INTERVIEWS, ALL OUR WORK—WILL GO TO HELP THE REPRESSION!

I KNOW, MITCH... I KNOW.

THAT NIGHT, LIU GANG AND I WERE SOMEWHERE IN BEIJING'S VAST SUBURBS, COLLECTING OURSELVES AND PREPARING FOR WHATEVER WAS NEXT. WHEN WE HEARD THE ARMY HAD ENTERED BEIJING, WE TRIED TO REACH THE SQUARE. OUR EFFORTS WERE IN VAIN.

ON JUNE 4, IN THE AFTERNOON, WE SPLIT UP. WANG JUNTAO AND CHEN ZIMING ORGANIZED ESCAPES FOR THE MOST WANTED ACTIVISTS: WANG DAN, LIU GANG, LAO MU, YANG TAO... NO ONE KNEW WHERE ANYONE ELSE WAS HEADED. WE EACH HAD TO GO OUR SEPARATE WAYS, TAKING EACH DAY AS IT CAME AND TRYING TO STAY OUT OF JAIL.

I HEADED OUT WEST, FOR THE MONGOLIAN PLAINS. ALL I HAD WITH ME WERE THREE ANTHOLOGIES OF POETRY AND CLASSICAL LITERATURE.

NOW AND THEN, I'D TUNE INTO THE BBC OR THE VOICE OF AMERICA. ONE DAY, I SAW ON THE TV THAT STUDENT LEADER YANG TAO HAD BEEN ARRESTED, TURNED IN BY THE HOTEL MANAGER WHO'D ALSO INFORMED ON LIU GANG.

I DIDN'T HAVE TIME TO BE SCARED. I HAD TO STAY FOCUSED, KEEP MOVING.

FOR A MOMENT, I IMAGINED SPENDING THE REST OF MY LIFE LIKE THIS, FLEEING TO THE REMOTEST CORNERS OF THE COUNTRY...

BZZZT BZZZT... FROM SYDNEY TO PARIS, LONDON TO *BZZZT...* MILLIONS OF PROTESTORS ARE DEMONSTRATING AGAINST THE REPRESSION UNDERWAY IN BEIJING. HOWEVER, THE COMMUNIST PARTY HAS PUBLISHED A LIST OF THE TWENTY-ONE RINGLEADERS IT IS CURRENTLY SEEKING...

FIVE OF THEM HAVE ALREADY MANAGED TO ESCAPE CHINA COVERTLY. STEPHANIE ANDREWS. BBC NEWS. HONG KONG.

95

AFTER SEVERAL WEEKS OF WANDERING, I REACHED LANZHOU. MY FRIEND HE YUAN TOOK A RISK PUTTING ME UP. I BEGAN TO CONSIDER THE POSSIBILITY OF CROSSING THE BORDER TO HONG KONG... THAT IS, IF I COULD MAKE IT 1000 MILES TO CANTON FIRST. AND SO, FAR AWAY FROM BEIJING, ON STATE TV, I STUMBLED UPON THE MOST EMBLEMATIC IMAGE OF TIANANMEN. WHICH THE STATE INTERPRETED IN ITS OWN WAY.

AND HERE WE HAVE PROOF OF THE COUNTER-REVOLUTIONARIES' ARROGANCE...

IN FACING THEM, OUR RESPECTFUL ARMY SHOWED REMARKABLE COMPOSURE.

NO ONE EVER FOUND OUT WHO THAT MAN WAS. IN A WAY, HE BECAME OUR UNKNOWN SOLDIER. IN THE EYES OF THE WORLD, HIS ACT SUMMED UP WHAT WE'D LIVED THROUGH AND WHO WE WERE. IN THE FACE OF AN ARMY, ALL WE HAD WAS OUR DETERMINATION, OUR YOUTH, AND OUR COMPOSURE. AND YET THAT IMAGE IS ALSO A LIE. IT WAS TAKEN ON JUNE 5, AFTER THE REPRESSION. IN REALITY, JUST A FEW HOURS EARLIER, THE TANKS HAD ROLLED RIGHT OVER THE STUDENTS.

FINALLY, ONE RAINY NIGHT, A SPEEDBOAT COLLECTED ME FROM THE CHINESE COAST.

SCANT MINUTES LATER, IT DROPPED ME OFF
ON A BEACH IN HONG KONG.

I WAS IN BRITISH TERRITORY.

JUST THEN, AS THE BOAT VANISHED INTO THE NIGHT, I REALIZED ITS
SPREADING WAKE WAS THE LAST THING CONNECTING ME TO CHINA.
SO I WATCHED UNTIL IT FADED COMPLETELY AWAY INTO THE PEARL
RIVER DELTA.

EPILOGUE

WITH THE HELP OF MANY ANONYMOUS CHINESE PEOPLE, PRO-DEMOCRACY ASSOCIATIONS IN HONG KONG, AND THE COOPERATION OF WESTERN GOVERNMENTS, SEVERAL DOZENS OF ACTIVISTS WERE ABLE TO FLEE CHINA FOR FRANCE.

I WAS ONE OF THEM. MANY OF THEM LATER HEADED TO THE U.S.

AS FOR ME, I PREFERRED TO TURN OVER A NEW LEAF IN THE LAND THAT HAD FIRST WELCOMED ME.

I LEARNED FRENCH. BECAME A UNIVERSITY PROFESSOR. TRAVELED A LOT. PUBLISHED BOOKS IN CHINESE AND FRENCH...

IT WAS FROM EUROPE THAT I NOW WATCHED CHINA AND THE GREAT UPHEAVALS OF HISTORY.

DIDEROT
1713-1784

I NEVER EXPERIENCED THE MOVEMENT'S FINAL HOURS, THE DEATH THROES OF TIANANMEN. IT'S BEEN THIRTY YEARS SINCE I LEFT CHINA... AND I'M NOT SURE THIRTY YEARS IS ENOUGH TO LEARN TO LIVE WITH SURVIVOR'S GUILT.

SOMETIMES, I THINK BACK TO THAT NIGHT IN LANZHOU, IN MY FRIEND HE YUAN'S APARTMENT.

OVER THE AIRWAVES, A VOICE FROM A FOREIGN STATION HAD INFORMED ME THAT PARIS WAS CELEBRATING THE BICENTENNIAL OF THE FRENCH REVOLUTION, WITH GUESTS FROM ALL OVER THE WORLD. THE GREAT CHINESE DRUM MEANT TO SYMBOLIZE THE LONG MARCH WAS PARADED DOWN THE CHAMPS-ÉLYSÉES, A SILENT SYMBOL OF THE SOLIDARITY OF THE FRENCH PEOPLE WITH THE VICTIMS OF THE REPRESSION.

"A NATION THAT GUNS DOWN ITS OWN YOUTH HAS NO FUTURE," PRESIDENT MITTERAND DECLARED.

ON THE BANKS OF THE YELLOW RIVER, MY TRANSISTOR RADIO PRESSED TO ONE EAR, I LEARNED THAT THE ENTIRE WORLD WAS SHOWING ITS SUPPORT FOR THE VICTIMS OF TIANANMEN, AND THAT A GREAT WIND OF FREEDOM WAS SWEEPING ACROSS THE PLANET THAT YEAR, IN 1989.

IN THE END, WE DID NOT FAIL.

THE SPRINGTIME THAT THE TANKS ROLLED OVER IN BEIJING WOULD FLOWER ELSEWHERE.

PARISER PLATZ, BERLIN. NOVEMBER 1989.

ON NOVEMBER 9, THE BERLIN WALL FELL, WITH NEITHER VIOLENCE NOR SHOTS FIRED. CHINESE PEOPLE WHO WERE THERE TOOK PART IN THE EVENT. THE GERMANS HAILED THEM AS BROTHERS, CONGRATULATING THEM FOR WHAT THEY'D SUFFERED AND ENDURED MONTHS BEFORE.

MAYBE THAT WINTER, XU FINALLY GOT TO SEE 99 BALLOONS TAKE FLIGHT WITHOUT SETTING OFF A WAR.

IN DECEMBER, ROMANIA PUT AN END TO CEAUȘESCU'S REGIME JUST AS CHILE DID TO PINOCHET'S.

THEN SOUTH AFRICA FREED MANDELA, AND BURIED APARTHEID.

IN THIS WAY, THE WORLD ENTERED THE FINAL DECADE OF THE MILLENNIUM.

HONG KONG

ON JUNE 4, 1990, A YEAR AFTER THE MASSACRE, 150,000 HONG KONG CITIZENS GATHERED IN SILENCE FOR A CANDLELIT VIGIL IN VICTORIA PARK.

AND FOR 30 YEARS, MORE THAN A HUNDRED THOUSAND PEOPLE HAVE GATHERED EVERY YEAR...

...TO KEEP THE FLAME OF TIANANMEN ALIVE.

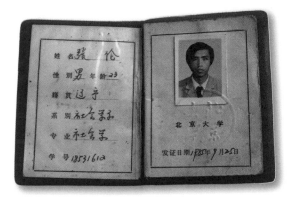

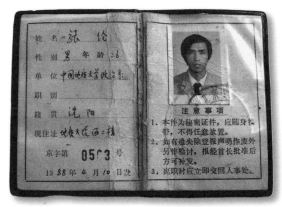

Before leaving Beijing in a hurry, Lun Zhang entrusted a friend with a few rare objects and souvenirs. They are reproduced on the endpapers of this book, and on the following pages.

In the late 1980s, the fledgling brand Meishi popularized western rolls. The packaging was inspired by American design. During the student movement, the people of Beijing would sometimes give these rolls to protesters at Tiananmen. Before my exile, I slipped the documents pictured here into one of these packages. I left it with my friend Xie Xiaoting, who took the risk of keeping it safe. A decade later, I recovered these souvenirs when they were mailed to me from the U.S., where my friend was a visiting professor.

A CHINESE CENTURY

(1919 – 2019)

In 1918, World War I came to an end. China had officially been a republic since 1911, after the revolution led by Sun Yat Sen. In reality, it belonged to local warlords squabbling with each other over territory.

1919
May 2-4: Demonstrations in Tiananmen Square against the transfer of German rights over Shandong to Japan, a decision made during the Versailles Peace Conference. These events come to be referred to as the "May Fourth Movement."

1921
July 1: The Chinese Communist Party (CCP) is founded with the support of communist Russia.

1931
September: Japanese troops invade Manchuria.

1934
October 14: The beginning of the Long March—369 days, 7460 miles—to escape the forces of the Kuomintang, the party in power since 1928 under the leadership of Chiang Kai-shek.

1937
November: Japanese troops take Nanjing and massacre 300,000 Chinese people.

1941
December 7: Japan attacks the American fleet in Pearl Harbor. War comes to the Pacific three years after starting in Europe.

Afterword

Since arriving in France, I have often heard Tiananmen spoken of as a great revolt. But to say so is to misunderstand history.

Naturally, our actions were the expression of a desire for democracy and freedom, of an urgent need to improve the conditions of daily life. However, by its very nature, the Spring of 1989 cannot be assimilated into the body of revolutionary imagery that has developed in the West. Our movement contained several highly specific elements that many foreigners were unable to percieve and many Chinese people have since forgotten.

"The revolution is not a dinner party," said Mao. When the people of China rise up, the means they employ are often violent. 1989 was a remarkable exception. Pragmatic and rational, the students knew that violence had no chance of succeeding. Above all, they had the nation's interests at heart, and wished to maintain stability, instead of plunging China back into the still-recent traumas of the Cultural Revolution. So it was that they found, in the hunger strike, a means of peaceful protest of a scope unprecedented in Chinese history.

Moreover, the demonstrations in Tiananmen Square and its subsequent occupation resulted from hopes that the Party's own policies had progressed. Endemic corruption, added to the stagnation of the reforms begun in the late 1970s, had stirred great frustration among the young.

▶

1945
August 6 and 9: Atomic bombs dropped on Hiroshima and Nagasaki. On August 15, Japan surrenders. Chinese casualties during the war number some twenty million. The civil war that will pit Communist forces against the Kuomintang's is in the offing.

1949
October 1: After defeating the Kuomintang, Mao Zedong proclaims the People's Republic of China in Tiananmen Square.

1950
February 14: Sino-Soviet Treaty of Friendship, Alliance and Mutual Assistance.
October: China goes to war with Korea to back the North and halt the advance of U.N. troops. The conflict will last three years.

1951
February 21: A campaign to eliminate counterrevolutionaries ushers in a series of movements intended to eradicate all who oppose the Party.

1956
January: Commercial and industrial enterprises in major cities are nationalized.

1957
April: The Hundred Flowers Campaign begins. The people, especially intellectuals, are encouraged to express their opinions of the Party openly. It is a brief period of freedom, immediately followed by violent repression.

1958
May 5-23: The Great Leap Forward begins. Mao attempts to relaunch the economy by relying on radical collective policies in the countryside. These policies, which remain in effect until 1961, lead to an economic collapse and a famine that will claim the lives of over 36 million Chinese people.

▶

In the mid-1980s, I had these student cards and a pin identifying me as a 3rd-year student at Peking University. Later these were replaced by a teacher card at the Chinese University of Geography. Rules under the photo on my professional ID card stress its value and strictly personal nature as a document. In the event of loss, I was to take out an ad in the paper stipulating that the card was now invalid, and request permission from my superiors to apply for a replacement.

1960
July 16: Political relations suspended between China and the U.S.S.R. The split between the two giants of communism is formalized.

1964
January 27: Official diplomatic relations established between France and the People's Republic of China.

1966
August: Liu Shaoqi is purged and Mao launches the Cultural Revolution. To consolidate his power, he makes young people and the Red Guard rise up against Party cadres and intellectuals.

1969
March 2: Skirmishes occur between Chinese and Soviet troops along the Ussuri River.
April 1: The CCP anoints Lin Biao as Mao's successor.
November 12: Liu Shaoqi dies in prison.

1971
April: Zhou Enlai welcomes the American ping-pong team to Beijing.
September 12: Lin Biao dies, allegedly due to a plane crash in Mongolia.
October 25: The People's Republic of China becomes a U.N. member.

1972
February 21-28: U.S. President Richard Nixon visits China.

1976
January 8: Death of Zhou Enlai, foremost representative of the Party's moderate wing.
April: Demonstrations, notably in Tiananmen Square, occur to honor Zhou Enlai's death and protest Mao's radical policies as carried out by the Gang of Four, led by Mao's wife Jiang Qing.
September 9: Death of Mao Zedong.
October 6: Gang of Four arrested.

1977
August: The Cultural Revolution officially comes to an end. Deng Xiaoping restores the Politburo Standing Committee of the Communist Party of China.

Thus, they were not seeking to overthrow those in power, but rather to urge them toward their stated goals of changing the regime in a peaceful, progressive manner. They wanted to be part of in-depth reform… or at least cooperate with the reformist wing within the Party. They were giving the Party a unique chance to transform itself, adapt its institutions to the needs of a society that was becoming ever more diversified in the wake of modernization. The Party was unable to seize this opportunity. The repression that ensued served to bury not only a movement, but also a chance for China to take a pivotal step in how it approached modernization.

Over the last few decades, some people have suggested that the tanks allowed China to maintain a climate of order and consistency conducive to its development. But just as the students never intended to cause chaos, so the repression failed to create the conditions for an economic emergence. In the last quarter-century, China has benefited from a favorable occurence—globalization—and followed a developmental model similar to those of Singapore, South Korea, and Taiwan. By closing off the political space in favor of a merely economic one, the repression in fact aggravated the inequalities inherent in this model and paved the way for a future where violence was more likely. Moreover, although inroads have been made in the areas of lifestyle and the economy, we must never forget that these too, owe a debt to the sacrifices made by the youth of 1989.

▶

1978
March: Formal adoption of the Four Modernizations.
November: The first posters appear on Beijing's Democracy Wall.
December: Official launch of the Reform and Opening Policy.

1979
January: Official diplomatic relations established between the U.S. and the People's Republic of China.
March 29: Wei Jinsheng arrested. Repression of the Democracy Wall movement begins.
July: The founding of the four "Special Economic Zones" occurs, an important measure in the process of opening up the economy.

1980
February 23-29: Zhao Ziyang and Hu Yaobang, supporters and initiators of economic reform and the Opening of China, join the Politburo Standing Committee. Rehabilitation of Liu Shaoqi.

1981
January 25: The Gang of Four goes on trial. Jiang Qing given a suspended death sentence.
June 27-29: Mao Zedong's place in history re-evaluated by CCP. Hu Yaobang made Secretary-General of the Central Secretariat.

1987
January 1: Student demonstrations in Tiananmen for reform and democracy occur.
January 16: Hu Yaobang resigns from the post of Secretary-General.
October 26: Zhao Ziyang becomes Secretary-General.
November 4: Li Peng is named Prime Minister.

1988
The reform of the price system leads to considerable inflation across the country. After rumors of shortages, people storm the shops.
June: The first national TV broadcast of the documentary series "Deathsong of the River."

▶

By chance, a telephone number and these Beijing bus
tickets were preserved in the slipcases of my cards. After
the movement began, I stopped taking the bus. In 1989, it
was still common practice to present ration tickets when
purchasing food. They were the last vestiges of the planned
economy in daily life.

1989

January: On the occasion of the 70th
anniversary of the May Fourth Movement,
33 intellectuals and scientists, including
astronomer Fang Lizhi, sign a petition
demanding amnesty for Wei Jingsheng
and human rights in China.
April 15: Death of Hu Yaobang.
April 22: Hu's funeral. 200,000 students
demonstrate in Tiananmen Square.
May 13: The hunger strike begins.
May 18: Zhao Ziyang purged.
May 21: The people of Beijing prevent the
army from entering the city.
May 31: Jiang Zemin is designated as the
new Party leader.
Night of June 3: Tanks enter Tiananmen.
Massacre occurs.

June 9: Deng Xiaoping gives speech
justifying the repression.
November 9: Deng Xiaoping announces
his "definitive retirement." Fall of the
Berlin Wall.

1990

January 10: Martial law is lifted in Beijing.

1991

December: The official end of the U.S.S.R.
Gorbachev resigns.

1992

January - February: Deng Xiaoping comes
out of retirement to relaunch reforms.
May 15: The Politburo Standing
Committee makes the transition to a
market economy official.

1993

September 20: Wei Jingsheng is freed.

1997

February 19: Death of Deng Xiaoping.
July 1 : Hong Kong returned to China,
followed by Macao two years later.

2001

December 11: China joins the World Trade
Organization.

Thirty years later, China is once more at the crossroads of history, with reform reaching a tipping point. Faced with rising social tensions, the Party could have taken a new step by going back to the policy reform process interrupted by the 1989 massacre.

Alas, Xi Jinping chose to go even farther back in time toward authoritarian measures left over from Maoism. In the short term, these measures may seem effective on the surface. But deep down, they will only exacerbate problems that have remained unresolved for the last 30 years, at the risk of compromising the fate of the nation and threatening worldwide stability.

What we stood for in 1989 is now more pertinent than ever. If China intends to build a peaceful and prosperous future, if it truly wishes to recover its past glory, it must return to Tiananmen and make a fresh start.

Lun Zhang, 2019

2002
November 15: Hu Jintao succeeds Jiang as Secretary-General of the Party.

2008
May 12: Earthquake in Sichuan: over 70,000 casualties reported.
August 8: The Olympic Games begin in Beijing.
December 10: On Human Rights Day, 303 intellectuals and activists, including Liu Xiaobo, sign Charter 08 calling for political reform: a guarantee of human rights, and the rehabilitation of Tiananmen victims.

2009
December 25: Liu Xiaobo is sentenced to 11 years in prison.

2010
May 1: Expo 2010, the World's Fair, opens in Shanghai.
October: Liu Xiaobo is awarded the Nobel Peace Prize.

2012
March: Bo Xilai removed as Party Chief of Chongqing on the heels of a violent power struggle within the CCP. He is sentenced to life in prison for corruption.
November: Xi Jinping becomes CCP Secretary-General.

2013
March: Xi Jinping becomes President of the People's Republic and launches a vast anti-corruption campaign.

2014
September - October: Massive protests in Hong Kong occur, known as the "Umbrella Movement," against Beijing policies regarding the democratic evolution of the former colony.

2017
July 13: Liu Xiaobo dies in prison.

2018
March: Xi Jinping amends the constitution, ending the limit on two consecutive presidential terms established under Deng Xiaoping and Jiang Zemin. In so doing, he paves the way for indefinite rule. On the 40th anniversary of the Opening of China, many voices, intellectuals among them, criticize the policies of those in power, calling for more comprehensive reforms.

■■■

This scarf was a special safe-conduct pass that allowed its bearer to travel between different zones of occupied Tiananmen Square. During a meeting, I asked the movement's main leaders to sign it. My own signature can be made out among those of Liu Xiaobo, Wu'Er Kaixi, Li Lu, Liu Suli, Liu Gang, Lao Mu, Zhang Boli, Yang Tao, Ma Shaofang, Shao Jiang, Chen Xiaoping, Fong Chongde, Zhou Dou, Wang Juntao, and Wang Dan. Chai Ling added a few humorous words about me: "Lun Zhang is a rascal."

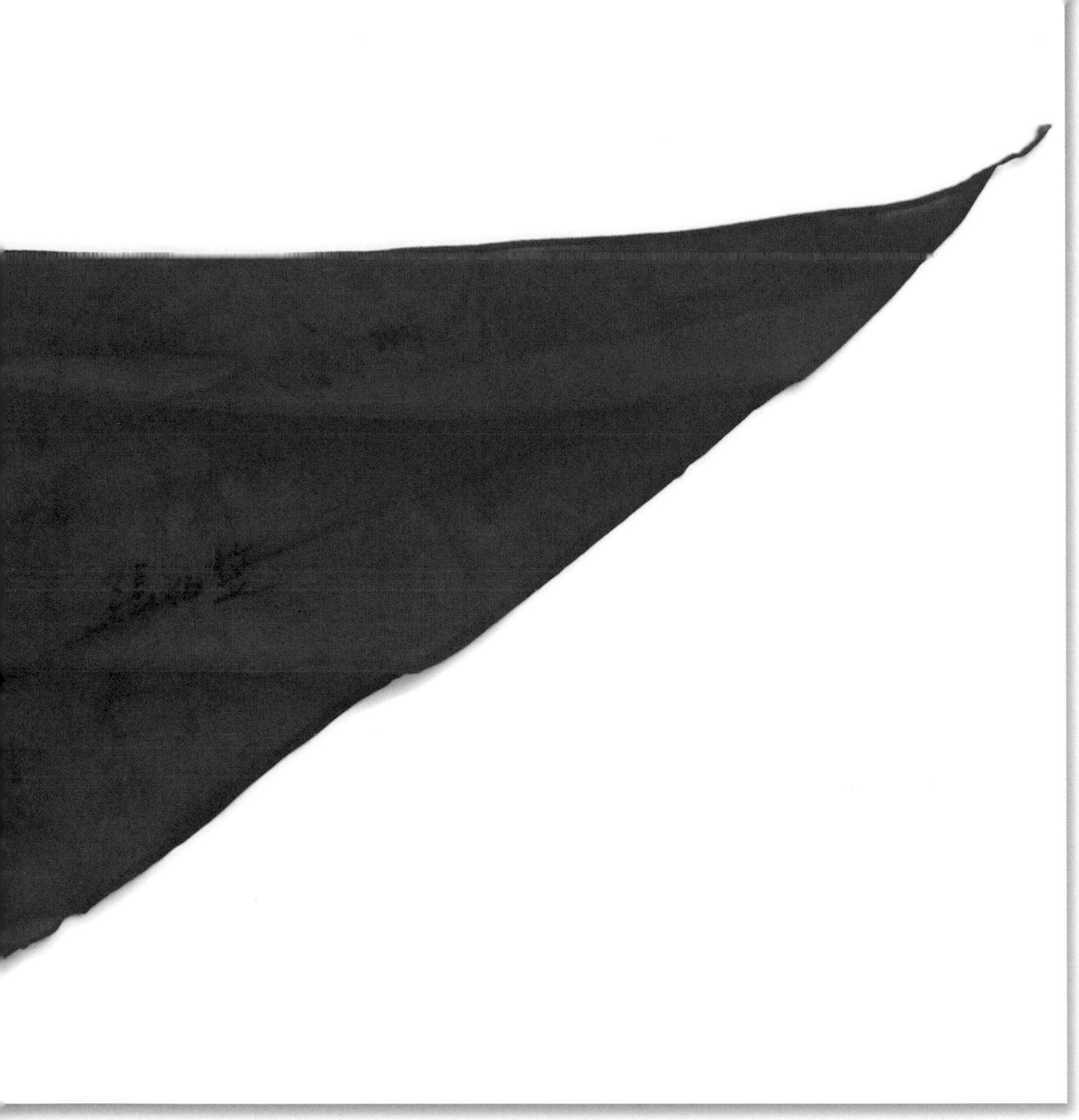

BACK COVER:
On April 16, 1990, shortly after I reached Paris, a painter friend of mine said he'd seen me on the French channel TF1. The night before, one year after Tiananmen, the evening news had re-broadcast images from the large demonstration in memory of Hu Yaobang. I did not come across this footage until 30 years later, while working on this graphic novel. Yes, that is indeed me wearing a banner asking Hu Yaobang's soul to return.

Acknowledgements

Lun Zhang

It is time I expressed my thanks to those who contributed to the making of this book. First of all, Anne Sastourné, a great editor at Le Seuil, whose idea it was to embark on this adventure. She spared no effort in ensuring it saw the light of day. Next, Adrien Gombeaud, a very talented writer. His pen, but also his heart, gave this story its shape. And last but not least, the imagination and talent of Améziane: the tragic scenes of these events are powerfully depicted. Louis-Antoine Dujardin spearheaded this project at Delcourt, lending his talent for organization, his great understanding, and his experience to see it through to its completion. To him I offer my sincere gratitude.

Adrein Gombeaud

I would like to thank everyone who opened the doors of this adventure to me: Anne Sastourné and Louis-Antoine Dujardin for their trust, Leslie Perreaut for her eyes, and of course, Amazing Améziane for his images. Special thanks to Lun Zhang for an unforgettable journey into the China of his memory. Lastly, thanks to Café Livre on Rue Saint-Martin for being so quiet on Monday mornings.

TRANSLATION BY **EDWARD GAUVIN**
LETTERS BY **FRANK CVETKOVIC**
EDITS BY **JUSTIN EISINGER** & **ALONZO SIMON**
DESIGN BY **CLAUDIA CHONG**

ISBN: 978-1-68405-699-6   23 22 21 20   1 2 3 4

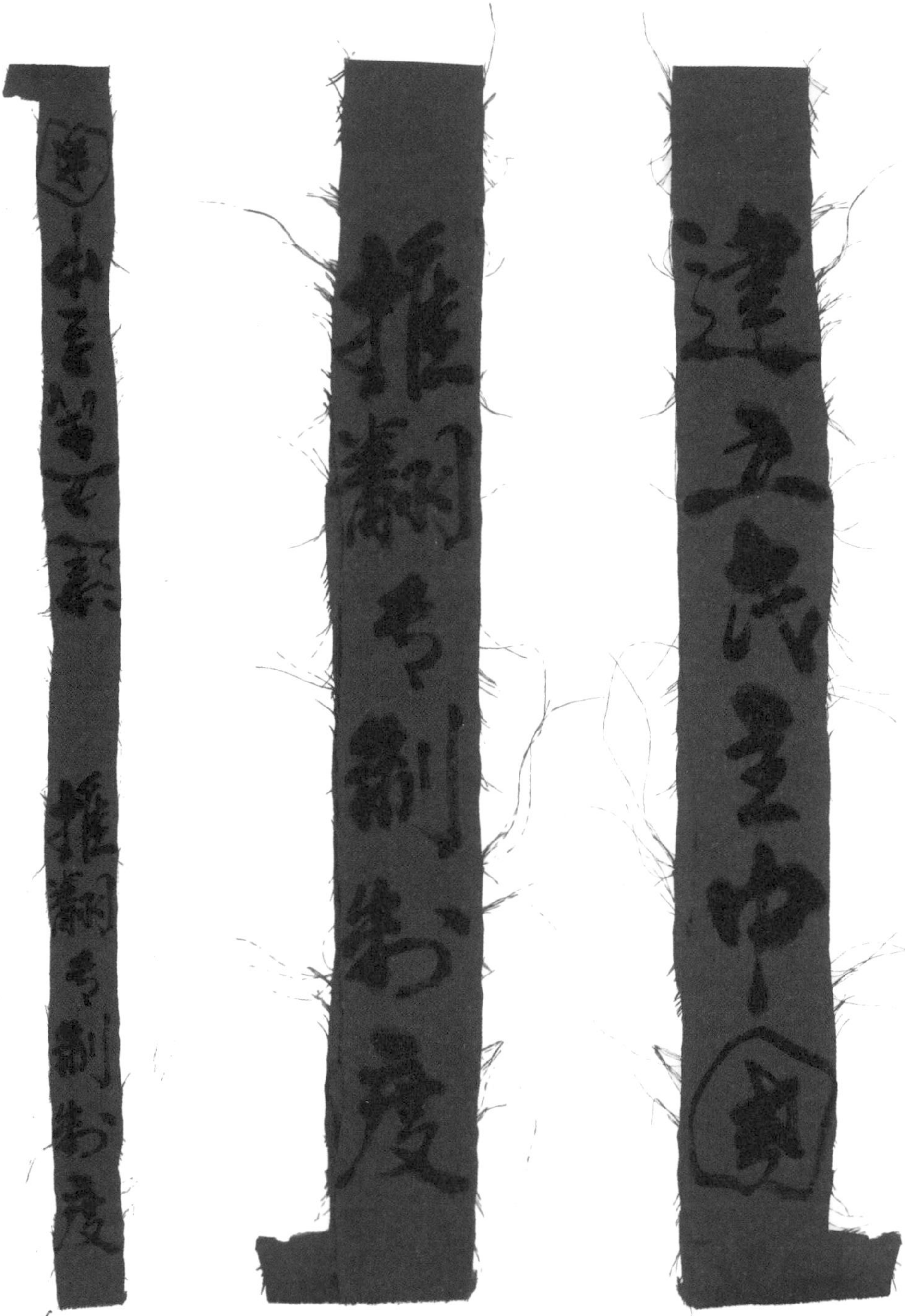
建立民主中国
推翻专制制度